DEPOSIT–REFUND SYSTEMS

DEPOSIT–REFUND SYSTEMS

Theory and Applications to Environmental,
Conservation, and Consumer Policy

PETER BOHM

Published for Resources for the Future, Inc.
By The Johns Hopkins University Press
Baltimore and London

Published for Resources for the Future
By The Johns Hopkins University Press, Baltimore, Maryland 21218

Library of Congress Cataloging in Publication Data

Bohm, Peter, 1935-
    Deposit-refund systems.

    Includes index.
    1. Deposit-refund systems. I. Resources for the future.
II. Title.
HC79.E5B63   351.82   81-47617
ISBN 0-8018-2706-X   AACR2

RESOURCES FOR THE FUTURE, INC.
1755 Massachusetts Avenue, N.W., Washington, D.C. 20036

Resources for the Future is a nonprofit organization for research and education in the development, conservation, and use of natural resources and the improvement of the quality of the environment. It was established in 1952 with the cooperation of the Ford Foundation. Grants for research are accepted from government and private sources only if they meet the conditions of a policy established by the Board of Directors of Resources for the Future. The policy states that RFF shall be solely responsible for the conduct of the research and free to make the research results available to the public. Part of the work of Resources for the Future is carried out by its resident staff; part is supported by grants to universities and other nonprofit organizations. Unless otherwise stated, interpretations and conclusions in RFF publications are those of the authors; the organization takes responsibility for the selection of significant subjects for study, the competence of the researchers, and their freedom of inquiry.

This book is a product of RFF's Quality of the Environment Division, Clifford S. Russell, director. Peter Bohm is professor of economics at the University of Stockholm, Sweden.

The book was edited by F. R. Ruskin and designed by Elsa Williams. The index was prepared by Florence Robinson, and the figures were drawn by Federal Graphics.

CONTENTS

FOREWORD

Over the past several years enthusiasm has been building in the United States for a series of political and administrative actions referred to collectively as "deregulation." In some areas, such as the airline and trucking industries, these actions involve the reduction of government's role as protector of monopoly or oligopoly positions. In other areas, such as environmental protection, a continuing government role as manager of common property resources is usually (but not always) acknowledged. Here the push for deregulation has often involved attempts to change the techniques used to achieve agreed-on goals rather than claims that there should be no government goals or interference. In particular, many people, both inside government agencies and in private interest and research groups, have advocated a reduction in the use of highly specific government commands directed at private (or lower jurisdictional) users of the environment—commands such as the specification of pollution control technology. Instead, the advocates of this sort of deregulation would have the government put into effect one or another economic incentive designed to encourage the desired sort of action without attempting to specify exactly what should be done.

The economic incentive systems that have received the most attention in the environmental literature have been effluent or emission charges and, more recently, marketable permits to pollute. This book is devoted to a different system—deposits and refunds. While familiar to us in several settings, deposit-refund systems turn out, as Bohm shows, to have promise for helping induce desired actions in several new environmental contexts. Indeed, such systems may be useful well beyond the field of environmental management. Thus, deposit–refund systems are potentially useful in three problem settings:

- when something is to be done that it would be desirable to see "undone" later, as with the purchase and subsequent return of bottles or of refrigeration units containing chlorofluorocarbons.
- when something might, but need not, happen that will result in social harm, for which the legal system cannot provide prompt or perhaps even eventual recovery, as with accidental chemical spills or bankruptcies of tour operators.
- when an action might, but need not, be taken that will result in social good, as with the maintenance of spare parts stocks for cars and appliances. (A deposit or performance bond would either guarantee refunds to consumers with appliances unrepairable because of a failure to continue making spare parts or would pay for continuing production by another company should the original manufacturer go out of business.)

In the first context, the deposit–refund approach seems natural, for the deposit is collected when the initial action is taken and the refund is obtained when it is "undone" as by return of empty bottles. In the other contexts, special charges or subsidies could also be used, and therefore it is useful to think about some of the special features of a deposit–refund system that might make that the preferred approach. One important distinction is between discouraging a class of actions and discouraging the undesirable after effects. In the bottle context this amounts to the difference between discouraging the use of bottles at all and discouraging their appearance as litter. It is usually the latter that we care about.

A second distinction involves who is out of pocket when. If, for example, a subsidy instead of a deposit–refund system were to be used to encourage spare parts maintenance, the government would have to raise the money for the subsidy elsewhere and would thus increase its budget or decrease some other service or payment. A deposit provides the money and the appliance maker pays the bill. Another distributionally important observation is that, in the case of consumer-paid deposits, the net incidence, after taking into account returns and hence refunds, may be such that poorer people are made relatively better off.

The third important distinction is between transferrable and nontransferrable incentives. A tax on bottles hits purchasers of bottles, but a deposit–refund system transfers the key incentive (to reduce litter) to anyone who happens to come upon a bottle "in the wild." There is another side to this feature: deposits may be paid to one set of stores and bottles returned to another set. Therefore any deposit–refund system with transferrable incentives requires a financial back-up system that transfers the deposits to the refunders.

As suggested by the above considerations, deposit–refund systems have some interesting properties, and Bohm's discussion of them is the latest in a series of RFF books that explore the use of economic incentives as tools of environmental policy. A pioneering work and one still widely used and quoted is *Managing Water Quality: Economics, Technology, Institutions* (1968) by Allen V. Kneese and Blair T. Bower. The economic incentive of most interest to these authors is the effluent charge, particularly as applied in water pollution control. The book *Environmental Improvement through Economic Incentives* (1977) by Anderson, and coauthors, also concentrates on effluent charges, but goes beyond economic properties to look at constitutional and political questions about their use as well as at practical matters such as monitoring. The most abstract and hence most general book of the series is that by Karl-Göran Mäler, *Environmental Economics: A Theoretical Inquiry* (1974). This work touches on all forms of incentive systems, and indeed, contains an interesting equivalence theorem: it is shown that there always exists a system of taxes and refunds that is equivalent to an "optimal effluent charge system" (pp. 238–239).

Bohm's book contains a mixture of theory and application that carries the reader from the foundations of deposit–refund systems to some exciting examples of their use. Along the way, Bohm shows how such systems can arise naturally in markets—without government intervention—as part of the endless campaigns of product and service differentiation. He also explains that features such as repurchase or trade-in allowances can usefully be thought of as deposit–refund systems. Within the broad category of government-initiated deposit–refund systems, he further distinguishes between consumer-paid and producer-paid deposits and indicates how the latter might even be used to provide performance incentives for government agencies. Having established the theory of deposit–refund systems, Bohm goes on to review the (sparse) empirical evidence on their effectiveness. His conclusions are necessarily tentative, but generally quite positive.

The final chapter of the book describes two potential applications of such systems: controlling the fate of the chlorofluorocarbons in refrigeration units, and encouraging maintenance of spare parts stocks for durable consumer goods. The reader will no doubt think of other possibilities. One such is as an innovation in the control of hazardous materials generally. Here, a deposit–refund approach would have the advantage of providing a continuing and decentralized incentive for users to keep track of materials. The existing, albeit new, U.S. system of "cradle-to-grave" control under the Toxic Substances Control and the Resource Conservation and Recovery acts, depends on sanctions to encourage the maintenance of an elaborate system of paper work. Many close observers and participants fear that this approach will prove extremely unwieldly, even unworkable.

Resources for the Future is pleased to publish this addition to the literature on economic incentives in environmental management. The tool of deposit–refund systems seems a most promising one, worth considering in many contexts and, indeed, of interest in many other areas of public policy as well. This book should therefore be of interest to students, researchers, and policy analysts with a variety of concerns.

May 1981   Clifford S. Russell
                                                    Resources for the Future
                                                    Washington, D.C.

PREFACE

Regulation seems to be the politician's primary answer to problems of resource allocation. Economic incentive systems are rarely chosen. There are at least two major reasons for this lack of practical interest in using economic instruments to guide decision makers in households, firms, and organizations. One is the governmental budget problems encountered—finding ways of financing subsidies, accepting unstable tax receipts—and another is the politically undesirable distributional effects that economic incentive systems are said to create. Here we deal with these aspects by analyzing a particular type of incentive system that tends to avoid some unwanted budgetary and distributional effects. The system is a package of policy instruments with two components: (1) taxes (deposits) on certain kinds of transactions, such as purchases of particular commodities, and (2) subsidies of (refunds for) particular forms of behavior with respect to consequences of the initial transactions. A simple illustration of the basic mechanism of this system (although the government is not financially involved in this instance) is a deposit on returnable beverage containers and a refund if the containers are returned instead of thrown away.

There are a number of existing or potential applications of such deposit–refund systems. In particular, when we observe that credit transactions may be an integrated part of the system, it is easy to find such applications. For example, different kinds of product guarantees and performance bonds can be regarded as versions of a deposit–refund system. A major purpose of this study is to analyze common features of such applications and to indicate further potential uses of the deposit–refund system, in particular for environmental, conservation, and consumer policy.

The emphasis of the study is on the principles and theory of deposit–refund systems rather than on applications and case studies. It should be pointed out, however, that the book is a collection of essays more than an integrated presentation with a unified mode of analysis. Chapter 2, which deals with market-generated deposit–refund systems, is a fairly technical discussion of issues in microeconomic theory. Chapters 3 and 4 elaborate the principal policy issues involved, with only a few brief sections of a more technical character. Chapter 5 describes and evaluates actual applications of deposit–refund systems. Finally, chapter 6 presents two potentially important applications that have not yet been tried. Thus the book contains sections for readers interested in economic theory and the principles of economic policy, as well as practical policy applications. To a large extent these sections may be read separately without too much inconvenience. (At least, so it appears to an optimistic author.)

In writing this book, I have benefited from helpful comments from many colleagues. Clifford S. Russell of Resources for the Future has given me constructive suggestions on several occasions. Mats Bohman, John Butlin, V. Kerry Smith, Raymond Kopp, Herbert C. Morton, Talbot Page, and John Sonstelie have read large parts or all of the manuscript and given me valuable comments. I have received constructive remarks from many others, in particular Jack Cumberland, Alan Krupnick, Karl-Göran Mäler, Julie Sundqvist, and Lewis Taylor. I am indebted to all of them.

Most of the work reported here was done while I was at RFF and at the Bureau of Business and Economic Research at the University of Maryland. I am grateful for the financial support and stimulating working conditions provided by both of these research organizations.

March 1981   Peter Bohm
                                                        University of Stockholm

DEPOSIT–REFUND SYSTEMS

1 INTRODUCTION

The use of economic incentive systems in public policy has been rather limited outside the sphere of stabilization policy. Despite economists' many arguments in favor of correcting market failures by introducing such systems,[1] few such proposals have been found politically acceptable. Instead, in areas such as environmental, conservation, and consumer policy, regulation has been the dominating policy instrument. This may be caused in part by a lack of sufficient understanding of incentive systems among politicians and bureaucrats. Direct regulation of the target variables is often intuitively easier to grasp than allocative taxes or subsidies, the effects of which are usually more indirect. For similar reasons, important long-term and other indirect effects of regulation often seem to be neglected by policy makers.[2]

One reason that policy makers avoid subsidies is, of course, their reluctance to have to raise additional government funds. Economic incen-

[1] For a recent presentation of such arguments directed to politicians and administrators, see Charles L. Schultze, *The Public Use of Private Interest* (Washington, D.C., Brookings Institution, 1977) and Frederick R. Anderson, Allen V. Kneese, Serge Taylor, Phillip D. Reed, and Russell B. Stevenson, *Environmental Improvements Through Economic Incentives* (Baltimore, Johns Hopkins University Press for Resources for the Future, 1978).

[2] For a discussion of these aspects as they relate to environmental policy, see William J. Baumol and Wallace E. Oates, *Economics, Environmental Policy and the Quality of Life* (Englewood Cliffs, N.J., Prentice-Hall, 1979).

tive schemes using taxes or fees would appear to be beneficial in such cases because they reduce reliance on general tax income, with its often distortive effects on resource allocation. However, incentive tax schemes may be technically impossible or administratively cumbersome and costly to effect. In addition, the distributional effects of taxes and charges are often disliked by government and by influential groups in society, so that the necessary political support cannot be mustered for this kind of policy.

In this book we discuss deposit–refund systems, a particular kind of economic incentive system that in many cases can replace pure tax or subsidy schemes as a policy alternative to regulation and at the same time avoid some of the undesirable distributional and budgetary effects of such schemes. A deposit–refund system is essentially a combination of a tax and a subsidy. To attain objectives in areas such as environmental, conservation, and consumer policy, a refund (subsidy) is offered to consumers or producers, or both, in order to stimulate activities that otherwise would not have been undertaken or to guide existing activities in time and space. For example, refund offers can be introduced to avoid having used objects such as beverage containers, discarded automobiles, and waste lubricating oil dumped in places where they would be harmful in one way or another. Or refund offers can be used as an instrument for reducing waste management costs to society and for recovering certain materials from waste when there are economies of scale in recovery operations or lags in adjustment of disposal behavior.

To avoid extensive distributional and budgetary effects and to create adequate incentives, the refund offer is coupled with a deposit (tax) that is introduced at an earlier point in the chain of transactions. Thus in a complete deposit–refund system the deposit is refunded if certain conditions are met by the decision maker. A complete deposit–refund system can now be seen to have a wider field of application than was suggested by the examples just given. The refunding of a deposit if a specific condition is met by the depositor provides an instrument for protecting certain rights that the government may wish to transfer to the buyers of a product. For example, deposits (or similar arrangements) made by producers could protect consumers from producers who fail to honor contracts or warranties because of bankruptcy. The system could also be used to correct for market failure in servicing consumer durables or in the provision of spare parts. It could be applied to help protect people from hazards that could arise from production sites left unattended after shutdown of production. In addition, deposit–refund systems could even be used to protect consumers of public services from unlimited delays or unfulfilled

Table 1-1. Examples of Policy Applications of Deposit–Refund Systems

Environmental policy applications	Conservation policy applications	Consumer policy applications	Other efficiency objectives
To prevent litter of containers, junked autos, tires, appliances	To encourage recycling of metals, paper, glass, lube oil	To protect guarantees and other contracts, such as: delivery contracts and guarantees on charter flights, construction work, repair services, consumer durables	To encourage efficiency in waste management, for example, by separating chemicals and toxic substances that otherwise cause high treatment costs
To prevent pollution by waste lube oil, mercury cells, PCB containers, nickel-cadmium batteries, cooling units		To ensure availability of service and spare parts	To correct market failure in second-hand, reuse, and scrap markets arising from inefficient pricing of primary products, economies of scale, lagging adjustment of disposal behavior
To encourage restoration of production, storage, and dump sites after shut-down		To protect against unknown hazards of new products	
		To protect against false sales claims	To encourage efficiency in government by encouraging timely processing of applications and claims and by ensuring scheduled completion of projects or promised delivery of services

promises of service delivery. This wide field of potential applications of deposit–refund systems will be explained in more detail throughout the discussion in the following chapters. Some of the major applications are briefly summarized in table 1-1.

DEPOSIT–REFUND SYSTEMS AND MICROECONOMIC THEORY

To create a unifying frame of reference, we introduce the deposit–refund mechanism into the context of conventional economic theory. Normally, it is sufficient to regard a commodity transaction as a simple exchange of a service—or a potential series of services embodied in a durable commodity—for a sum of money. This two-dimensional, price–quantity relation, however, overlooks certain aspects of real-world transactions that may be of crucial importance in specific applications of the theory. Thus in exchange for the price, the buyer may get a more or less extensive set of rights (and liabilities), such as a guarantee of servicing of the product bought, a replacement or money-back guarantee if the product is faulty, and a right to return the product when it is worn out. Or, in the case of rental systems, the buyer will have to return the product at the end of the service period he has paid for or agreed to pay for. In some cases, additional payments are required if the buyer does not comply with the set of conditions established at the time of the purchase. Or, if he uses certain rights instead of others, the buyer may be paid for doing so; that is, he may be refunded a part of the price originally paid for the commodity.

Such a package of conditions, specifying buyer and seller rights and liabilities and possibly including rates for certain contingency payments, can be shaped by the market—it may be part of the product differentiation established by the market, or a product package produced by all sellers in a market may be the outcome of competition among different versions of the product package. A market-generated producer guarantee attached to a product is one such example. In other cases, however, the origin of the product package is found in the law or other forms of government intervention. The government may have specified certain minimum rights for the consumer, such as the right to compensation for a deficient product, a standardized guarantee for a type of product, or a free pick-up service for worn-out hazardous products. In certain cases the government may also have specified the payments to be made when certain rights are used. For example, there may be rules for minimum compensation to buyers of faulty products or minimum deposit (refund) laws such as those for beverage containers in certain areas (see chapter 5).

In other words, we can regard a government-initiated deposit–refund system as an instrument shaping the product package exchanged in a market. The consumer may be given the right to a refund if he returns a waste product or a faulty product to the seller. For this right, the consumer may have had to pay a formal deposit at the time of the purchase of the product or, which amounts to the same thing, he may have merely paid a higher product price. A producer may also be given such rights and liabilities under similar conditions, that is, as a buyer of certain inputs. But, in addition, he may be required to pay a deposit to the government to ensure that he fulfills certain conditions established in contracts with buyers or a third party; for example, to ensure that production sites are restored after production has ceased or that guarantees are protected in case of bankuptcy. Such cash deposits may be replaced by a bank guarantee or an insurance policy without any change in the basic characteristics of the deposit–refund system.

DEPOSIT–REFUND SYSTEMS AND ALTERNATIVES

In some cases a deposit–refund system may be the only possible policy solution. For example, it is hardly likely that the authorities could catch a significant number of those people who throw away small hazardous products such as cadmium batteries and thus damage the environment. Therefore, neither a ban nor a tax on improper disposal could be expected to work in this case. In contrast, a deposit on the sale of such batteries and a refund for properly returned batteries could be designed to provide appropriate incentives to protect the environment.

To cite another example, assume that 90 percent of a returnable commodity or a kind of scrap is returned without the support of any government initiative. To introduce a subsidy to increase this figure to, say, 100 percent would rarely be worthwhile, given the "costs" of having to finance the subsidy of those 90 percent already being returned. Thus, to get the remaining 10 percent of the units returned, the actual cost would be the social costs of the total volume of subsidies. This cost may be too high for whatever increased returns are desired, and it has consequently been used as an argument against such subsidies.[3]

A deposit–refund system could accomplish the same thing that a subsidy would, but at a much lower social cost. Those who already return their units will pay and receive the same amount (an appropriate rate of interest may be paid to the depositor, of course), and so no cost other than that of temporary forced saving in the amount of the deposit will hit them. The cost to the people who are not already returning their units will be the inconvenience of using this disposal alternative (in addition to the probably negligible cost of forced saving). But it will not cost the

[3] See, for example, Resource Conservation Committee, *Choices for Conservation* (Washington, D.C., U.S. Government Printing Office, 1979) p. 100.

government anything more than the administrative effort. Thus, if administrative costs and inconvenience costs are small enough, it may pay to have recovery rates increased in this way.

In other cases a deposit–refund system may be the only realistic way to introduce economic incentives; hence it may be the only alternative to regulation. Assume, for example, that government would like to consider making those who burn oil and release sulfur dioxide into the atmosphere pay for their sulfur emissions. A charge on all actual emissions would presumably be ruled out because of prohibitive measurement costs. In contrast, an economic incentive system could be introduced consisting of a deposit on the sulfur content of the fuel and a refund on the sulfur recovered.[4] For firms to qualify for refunds at rates far above the market price for sulfur, the authorities may in some cases need to check actual oil purchases and verify the existence of sulfur recovery devices. The control costs would still be small in comparison with the costs of administering a tax on sulfur emissions.

As was pointed out earlier, deposit–refund systems may provide the same economic incentives as taxes or subsidies and at the same time avoid some of the disadvantages of these alternatives. That deposit–refund systems have the same incentive effects is clear from the fact that the deposit becomes a fee if the decision maker's behavior does not qualify for a refund. In certain applications, such systems may provide stronger or more well-focused incentives or involve a smaller amount of policy costs (administrative, enforcement, and information costs) than alternative solutions. For example:

1. If a commodity on which a deposit has been paid is disposed of in a way that does not qualify for a refund, someone else may take care of it and get the refund; this would not happen with regulations or fees on an improper disposal.
2. In a deposit–refund system the owner of a commodity has an incentive to prove that the commodity has not been disposed of in an improper fashion; in alternative systems the owner may have an incentive to hide the fact that it has been disposed of in an improper fashion.
3. In some cases it is simpler and less expensive to administer deposit–refund systems in which one is paid for choosing a certain kind of

---

[4] A deposit–refund proposal along these lines was made by a Swedish government committee (Miljökostnadsutredningen) in 1976. The proposal was never accepted by the Swedish parliament.

activity or disposal than systems in which one has to pay for alternative kinds of activity or disposal.

4. It may be simpler in some cases to formulate the conditions under which there is a refund than to state the conditions under which it is forbidden to dispose of the commodity or under which there is a fee for doing so.

5. By paying a deposit or by being told about the refund prospect by the seller as a sales argument, the buyer or user is informed about the conditional refund and thus about (maximum) liability; making similar information available and effective is usually quite costly under alternative systems.

6. The collection costs in deposit–refund systems may in some cases be lower than the corresponding costs under a regulatory system or a system of charges that, to be effective, may require extensive checking operations, prosecution, and so on (see the cadmium battery example mentioned earlier).

Thus policy costs may be lower for deposit–refund systems than for alternative solutions. In addition, budgetary effects of deposit–refund systems may be more attractive to policy makers. Whereas subsidies and regulations with high policy costs create a need for additional government funds, and charges or other allocative taxes may be disliked by administrators when they give rise to an unstable volume of government revenue, deposit–refund systems tend to leave the budget intact to the extent that refunds (paid by the government) approach the volume of deposits (directly or indirectly paid to the government).

Because distributional considerations play a fundamental role in economic policy, such aspects of deposit–refund systems should be discussed in some detail at this point. Let us focus on a deposit–refund system designed to influence disposal behavior in order to reach a given policy goal. In the case in which refunds are set at a level such that a maximum return rate is achieved—say, all beverage containers are returned for a refund by the original buyers—there will be no effects on the net *money income* distribution.[5] In the case in which less than a maximum return rate is achieved, the return rate may differ among income groups; for example, it may be higher for households with a low opportunity cost for time, that is, for low-income households. This means that the deposit–

---

[5] Although the more relevant concept—the welfare or real income distribution—often will be affected in such a case, it is likely to be less tangible and therefore of less concern to politicians.

refund system would have a progressive distributional effect for deposits on commodities with unitary income elasticity. In contrast, a product charge or any other policy alternative of an excise tax type—say, in the amount of the expected average negative environmental effect—would be proportional to income under the same circumstances. It would, moreover, definitely raise commodity prices and so, for example, definitely hit households at or below the poverty line. And it would hit those who buy inexpensive versions of the affected commodity harder, relatively speaking, than those who buy luxury versions. Apart from the effects on different income groups, product charges would not differentiate between "bad" and "good" behavior, such as littering and nonlittering, and thus would not be as equitable as a refund would, in the normative sense implied here. Finally, the deposit informs the buyer about different disposal options and their costs at the time of purchase, in contrast to a tax on a nonreturn option or a subsidy on a return option, neither of which it is relevant to observe until the time of disposal. This increase of the information level in the economy could benefit, in particular, households that are uninformed because of poor education. This may be another distributional aspect of concern to politicians.

The basis for the analysis that follows can be found in what we have now suggested, that is, that deposit–refund systems can provide economic incentives that are compatible with social efficiency and have at the same time budgetary and distributional effects that may be politically acceptable.

OUTLINE OF THE DISCUSSION

In this study, deposit–refund systems will be analyzed in general terms as well as in various specific applications to attain policy goals such as (1) environmental protection, (2) recovery of materials, and (3) consumer protection.

Chapter 2 deals with deposit–refund systems as they can be expected to be generated by the market forces in the economy. Here we discuss in particular the effects of such systems on consumer and producer behavior and on market prices. The presentation in this chapter is fairly condensed and technical. The reader who is primarily interested in policy issues may read only the introductory and the summary sections of this chapter and proceed to chapter 3.

In chapter 3 we begin to analyze policy issues for which deposit–refund systems can be useful. The emphasis in this chapter is on consumer-paid deposits and on the overall effects on the economy of such deposit–refund systems.

Chapter 4 contains a similar discussion of producer-paid deposits and entails a shift of focus from environmental and conservation policy to issues primarily relevant for consumer policy. In this chapter we also discuss whether or not deposit–refund systems in particular versions can be applicable within the public sector.

In chapter 5 we analyze some of the existing empirical evidence on government-initiated deposit–refund systems—beverage containers and junked cars (consumer-paid deposits without and with financial government involvement, respectively) and waste lubrication oil and package tours (producer-paid deposits with and without cash payments, respectively). The reader who is primarily interested in practical applications or wants to study such applications prior to a discussion of the theoretical issues may proceed directly to chapter 5.

In chapter 6 we discuss in some detail two possible applications of deposit–refund systems that have not been used so far—consumer-paid deposits on cooling equipment (for environmental protection, conservation, and efficient waste management) and producer-paid deposits or credit versions thereof to guarantee the availability of spare parts on certain durables (for consumer protection).

As has already been indicated, readers with different interests may approach this book in different ways. The reader who is interested in the theoretical aspects of market-generated and government-initiated deposit–refund systems should read the chapters in the order in which they are presented and may wish to take only a brief look at the applications in chapters 5 and 6. The reader with an interest mainly in the policy aspects of these systems should skip chapter 2, except perhaps for its introductory and summary sections; he may also wish to avoid the details in the section "Effects of Consumer-paid Deposits" in chapter 3. Finally, the reader whose interests focus on the applications of deposit–refund systems could read the summaries of chapters 2 through 4 and read chapters 5 and 6, disregarding the references to the presentation earlier in the book that appear in these last two chapters.[6]

[6] Much has been written about beverage container deposits, but deposit–refund systems in general seem to have received little attention. A general reference can be made to textbooks on environmental economics, such as that by Baumol and Oates,

MAJOR CONCLUSIONS

1. Deposit–refund systems are much more widespread and general in concept and in practice than is normally assumed.

2. Market-generated systems, such as producer-initiated refund offers, may arise from attempts to increase product demand or reduce costs of production, or both. The introduction of refund offers does not always increase product prices (where prices are defined to include deposits wherever deposit payments are specified).

3. The reasons why a government may want to establish a deposit–refund system can go beyond and be different from the reasons why markets automatically establish such systems. A government may want to intervene in market-generated systems as well as introduce deposit–refund systems in markets where no such systems otherwise would exist. In the former case, for example, systems for beverage containers that arise spontaneously from market forces are unlikely to be Pareto optimal.

4. Government-initiated deposit–refund systems may originate from social efficiency considerations—on which the main emphasis is placed here—or from merit want aspects.

5. Under efficiency-based systems, refund rates reflect the value of external effects avoided, a shadow price of exhaustible resources, or the incentive reinforcement required for attaining a long-run optimal position.

6. Deposit–refund systems may involve deposits paid by consumers, producers, or government branches. In all cases, policy goals require in general that the (central) government, directly or indirectly, collect the deposits and finance the refund payments.

7. Producer-paid deposits are likely to be replaced by purchases of bank guarantees, which will improve the overall efficiency of the

---

Economics, Environmental Policy and the Quality of Life, chapter 17. One of the more comprehensive studies of beverage container deposits can be found in the Organization for Economic Cooperation and Development (OECD) publication, *Beverage Containers—Reuse or Recycling* (Paris, 1978). See also the report by the Resource Conservation Committee, *Choices for Conservation*. For applications to the field of consumer policy very little seems to be available. A study of issues related to the discussion of product guarantees below can be found in Geoffrey Heal, "Guarantees and Risk-Sharing," *Review of Economic Studies*, vol. 44 (October 1977) pp. 549–560.

deposit–refund system. Producer profits do not always decrease as a result of the introduction of such systems by the government.

8. Government-paid deposits would in general be replaced by rules for financial responsibility of the government agency involved. Experiments are called for to test the applicability of financial government-to-government or government-to-consumer liability.

9. There is empirical evidence of successful applications of deposit–refund systems to beverage containers, waste lubrication oil, and junked cars and for the protection of consumers of charter flight packages. However, significant improvements in the actual applications appear to be possible in most of these cases. Thus a socially efficient system for containers seems to require that at least part of the deposits be paid indirectly to the government. And in the case of junked cars, it has proved to be necessary to avoid rigid refund rates in order to maintain the incentive effects under inflationary conditions.

10. Overall, deposit–refund systems seem to be a neglected policy approach to serious environmental problems and to problems of consumer protection.

2 MARKET-GENERATED DEPOSIT–REFUND SYSTEMS

INTRODUCTION

Refund offers made by firms can be regarded as versions of general deposit–refund systems. Such market-generated systems may be introduced and administered by the producers or the sellers of a product. As we indicated in chapter 1, disposal options as well as product guarantees and other extensions of buyer rights can be seen as particular kinds of refund systems. For example, consumers may be given the right to return a refrigerator (1) within a week at no cost other than handling and transportation costs (a "cooling-off" period), (2) within a year at no cost whatever provided certain faults in the product have appeared (a free-replacement or money-back guarantee), or (3) within, say, a ten-year period at a given indexed return price, or a free-of-charge pickup (a disposal option). Or conditions (2) and (3) may relate to an easily detachable part of the refrigerator, say the refrigerant coil (which may be the result of an induced redesign of the product).[1]

The value of the refund to the buyer may deviate significantly from the seller's expected costs for this set of rights. The refund value can be seen to equal the price net of return costs under condition (1), the price

---

[1] What happens in case of seller bankruptcy is disregarded here but discussed at length in chapter 4. The particular application to refrigerators and other types of cooling equipment is analyzed in some detail in chapter 6.

or the resale price under condition (2), and the return price under condition (3). Under other conditions, no refund would be offered, and no return automatically accepted. This does not, of course, preclude the possibility that consumers may resell the commodity to someone else or to the seller in a transaction that is voluntary for both parties.

Some refunds may in practice be such that they only equal and may even fall short of a rebate that is offered to those buyers of new products that do not bring any trade-ins or other product returns. We avoid dealing with such cases here by assuming that the price of a new product is the same for both categories of buyers and thus that the refund always is a real, not a nominal, payment.

In this chapter we deal exclusively with market-generated refund systems. One purpose is to show some of the implications of such systems, in particular those implications that reappear in a government-initiated deposit–refund system. Another is to clarify the difference between a refund system that is imposed by law but that the government is not financially involved in and a deposit–refund system with a government-owned deposit part. And it should be noted that governments not only may initiate new deposit–refund systems but also may intervene in existing market-generated ones.

We start by discussing possible motives for market-generated refund systems. After that we study the effects of such systems on the buyer's disposal behavior and product demand. The behavior of the producer introducing the refund offer is analyzed in the section "The Producer Decision." In this section we discuss the choice of refund rates and prices as well as the choice of refund conditions and product design. The main results are summarized in the final section. Sections of this chapter that can be skipped without losing track of the main argument are indented and in smaller type.

MOTIVES FOR MARKET-GENERATED REFUND SYSTEMS

Producers and sellers (hereinafter producers, for convenience) may introduce refund offers for a number of reasons. Assuming that producers want to maximize profits, we expect all these reasons to be different ways of contributing to this goal. Two main avenues can be distinguished: measures that increase demand for the product, probably at a cost, and measures that aim at a reduction of production costs. More specifically, a refund offer may refer to a part of a product having an expected durability that far exceeds that of the rest of the product, assuming that the existing product design is more profitable than other designs, such as those in which all parts have the same expected durability. It may even refer to a product or a set of products as a whole whose durability exceeds the period for which (many) consumers expect to use it. In this case the deposit–refund system will be recognized as an ordinary rental system (where the ownership remains with the seller). However, we here abstract from this extreme case, which in general will be one where all consumers return the commodity for a refund without considering alternative ways of "disposing" of it.

In all the market-generated systems it is implicit that the expected costs of handling and reusing the returnable part or product are lower than the expected overall revenues to the producer. Now, it is quite common in practice—the guarantee case being a good example—that such revenues need not emanate from an actual reuse of the returned item. Firms may simply have found (or merely believe) that an offer to pay "$A for your old Y when you buy a new Z" is an effective marketing device to speed up replacements in order to increase sales and profits. Actually, this is an instance in which refunds to some consumers (old customers) could work as a profitable price discrimination device.[2] Thus the old Y may be simply dumped as waste or at least not have a reuse or scrap value exceeding $A. The same is true, of course, for trading stamps, coupons, and other artificial "parts" added to the product merely as a return instrument. In all these cases the difference between the refund and the actual reuse value will represent a reduction of the producer's net price for the group of old customers in relation to the price paid by others. This result is illustrated for a monopoly in figure 2-1, where the net reuse value V is assumed to be zero and marginal costs (MC) are constant. Here optimal price is increased from p_1, where no price discrimination is taking place, to p_2, with $p_2 - R$ being the price net of refunds (R) for old customers, all of whom are assumed to return their used products as soon as $R > 0$.

---

[2] For a discussion of this issue, see B. F. Massell and R. M. Parish, "Empty Bottles," *Journal of Political Economy*, vol. 76 (November/December 1968) pp. 1224–1233. We note, in addition, that a producer may prefer a temporary refund offer to a temporary price reduction in order to stimulate demand in a market that is believed to be sluggish for a short period only. The reason may be that the producer wants to avoid outright price competition (for example, in an oligopolistic market) or simply that he wants to avoid frequent price changes.

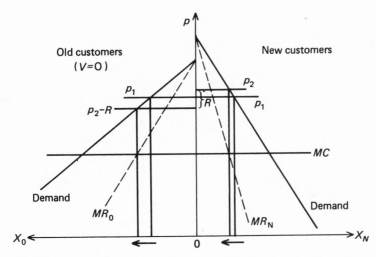

Figure 2-1.

It is only when the reuse or scrap value exceeds \$$A$ that there is reason to believe that physical reuse is a motive for the offer to accept returns. It should be noted, however, that price discrimination may remain as a motive in this case, too, if the refund still could be used as an effective price discrimination instrument. A firm with a monopoly position in the market for new products would benefit from this type of price discrimination even when demand, *ceteris paribus,* is less price-elastic for old customers than for new customers, which, in fact, may be the most interesting case. This is illustrated in figure 2-2, where $V > 0$ and where old customers have the least price-sensitive demand in contrast to the case of figure 2-1. Here $MR_0 + V$ represents the net marginal revenue from old customers. This will be made equal to MC if the price is reduced from p_1 to p_2, which will also make marginal revenue from new customers MR_N equal to MC. Here the refund is such that MC equals $MR_0 + V$ at $p_2 - R$, the net price for old customers. In this case, the refund is obviously smaller than the reuse value.

Aside from price discrimination and product reuse, we have the case in which risk aversion makes it profitable for both producers and (at least some) buyers to have product risks transferred to the producer side of the market, that is, to the party with the most information and the party most capable of risk pooling. To be more specific, the risk for product failure is likely to make a number of consumers abstain from buying the product. The producer, knowing more about the frequency of product failure than the consumer, could introduce a product guarantee

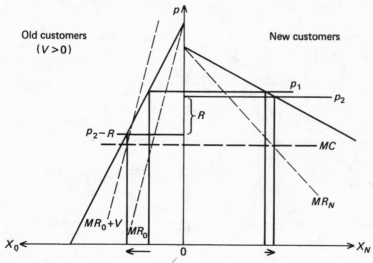

Old customers
$(V > 0)$

New customers

Figure 2-2.

and add an "insurance premium" to the product price and still get a net increase in demand due to consumer risk aversion. This is true in particular when moral hazard is not an important phenomenon, that is, when the buyer's behavior is not affected by the product guarantee so as to increase risks for product failure.

For any of the reasons now mentioned, producers may offer a conditional refund on their products or on certain parts of them. As we have indicated, the refund conditions may be quite strict, limiting not only the time and place of the return but also the kind of purchases the refund may be used for. However, strict qualifications in these respects do not exist in all market-generated deposit–refund systems. For example, firms producing similar products may decide to pay refunds on all brands in the industry, thus widening the terms of refund both geographically (sellers other than the original one offer refunds) and with respect to the acceptable uses of the refund. Or refunds may be offered for all returns without any ties on the use of the refund. This may be the case, for example, when standardized containers are used in the industry and used containers have a reuse value.

From the point of view of our ultimate interest in the policy aspects of deposit–refund systems, it is important to note the relevance of the type of market-generated refund offers discussed here. The fact that such offers actually are made suggests, first of all, that deposit–refund systems exist in many areas and may be much more common than is evident at first glance. Second, the existence of return options implies that collection activities are actually going on in the market economy and that costs for these are not prohibitive. This is important to note when, for example, there are policy reasons for considering new ways of dealing with products that already are being returned (cooling equipment may be one such example; see chapter 6).

EFFECTS OF REFUND OFFERS ON BUYERS

In some of the existing producer-initiated deposit–refund systems, the refund is not predetermined in the sense that its existence or size is known at the date of the original purchase. In such cases the effects are similar to those of a secondhand or scrap market, which has market-determined prices. That is to say, the spot refund or the spot resale value affects the decision of what to do with a used product at each point in time just as a predetermined refund would do, *ceteris paribus,* but the impact at the time of the original purchase is probably quite different from what we expect from a system with predetermined refund rates. Although the consumer may behave as if he is taking the expected resale or refund value into account at the time of the purchase, hence allowing us to treat predetermined and market-determined spot refunds in a similar fashion, we must observe the possibility of a more fundamental difference between the two cases. As the opposite extreme to treating them as identical, we shall take the non-predetermined case to mean that future resale or refund possibilities have no effect at all at the time of the purchase, although expected resale or refund values are positive. The refund or resale price can in this case be approximated by the certainty-equivalent price of zero.

Because there may be particular conditions attached to a predetermined refund offered by producers, uncertainty will arise in this case as well, if these conditions or their relevance is unknown to the consumer when he buys the product. In particular, when the refund offered is tied to a renewed purchase from the same firm, it will typically be uncertain at the time of the first purchase whether or not the purchaser wants to buy a product from this firm at a later stage. Whenever there are substantial uncertainties of this kind, we may assume as an extreme case that no tied refund offer, not even a predetermined one, would affect the decision of whether or not to make a first purchase. Thus from an analysis point of view we end up with two cases, one in which the refund offer affects the initial decision of whether or not to buy the product as well as, at a later time, the decision of whether or not to return it in a way that makes the consumer eligible for the refund, and another in which the refund affects only the latter decision. With respect to product guarantees we might note that the latter decision should be rather trivial in most cases. That is to say, if the product breaks down in a way that is covered by the warranty, we expect the consumer to return the product. Thus for product guarantees it is only the effects on demand of the product that seem to require a more detailed analysis (see the section "Other Producer Decision Variables" in particular).

Against this background it is natural to separate the effects of refund offers into (1) an effect on the disposal (resale) decision and (2) an effect on the purchase decision. We deal with the two in turn.

The Disposal Decision

In this section we analyze how the introduction of a refund offer affects the consumer's decision of (1) whether, at the time of product disposal, to dump the product or return it for a refund, and (2) whether, at each point in time, to keep the product or dispose of it. We also look into the effects resulting from changes in the constraints on the consumer's refund use.

The case in which a refund offer does not affect the decision of whether or not to buy a product is analytically identical to the case in which a refund offer is unexpectedly introduced on products in current use. We study consumer behavior in this case in two steps, as just indicated. First, the consumer may choose between two ways of getting rid of the product: he may dump it at an imputed cost of $C_d \geq 0$, or he may return it at a refund R (with no ties) and at an imputed cost of $C_R \geq 0$. Second, the consumer chooses between disposing of the product and keeping it. In principle, the latter decision is influenced by the choice of disposal alternative.

These two decisions can be studied under many alternative sets of assumptions. Here we shall use a set of simple assumptions that seem to be particularly relevant for the subsequent policy discussion. We assume that

1. C_d and $C_R - R$ are (made) known and are taken to be constant over time; thus regardless of the exact date when actual disposal

occurs, it is known in advance which disposal alternative will be used, depending on whether C_d exceeds or falls short of $C_R - R$.

2. The consumer will eventually stop using the product and dispose of it; formally, we assume that the consumer in period t has a net benefit, $v(t) - C_u(t)$, from using the product, known to be nonincreasing over time; $v(t)$ is the gross benefit from using this particular item in period t, and $C_u(t)$ are the costs attached to use or nondisposal, such as storage, of the product in that period. (If $v(t) - C_u(t)$ is constant, it is assumed to bè so only for a finite number of periods. Thus durability of the "one-hoss-shay" type, that is, constant physical characteristics of the product up to a certain point in time when it "falls to pieces," can be regarded as a special case covered by this assumption.)

Now, the consumer in the situation presented here will eventually return the product or the refund-eligible part of the product, if $C_R - R < C_d$, that is, if net return costs fall short of costs of dumping. And he will actually do so today (t) if it does not pay him to keep the product, that is, if the net benefit value or net use value, $v(t) - C_u(t)$, falls short of the gain from disposing of the product in this period instead of waiting one more period. In other words, he will return the product at time t if

$$v(t) - C_u(t) < -\min(C_d, C_R - R) + \frac{1}{1 + r_c} \min(C_d, C_R - R)$$

$$= -\frac{r_c}{1 + r_c} \min(C_d, C_R - R) = \frac{r_c(R - C_R)}{1 + r_c}$$

whenever $R - C_R > -C_d$. Here r_c is the consumer's rate of discount for returning the product in the next period. Note that the left-hand side of this inequality reflects his valuation of keeping this particular item of the product. Thus in case he would buy a new item of the same product once he has disposed of the old one, $v(t) - C_u(t)$ will reflect his net use value of keeping the old item for one additional period (see the literature on durability for details on such computations[3]).

---

[3] See, for example, Teddy Su, "Durability of Consumer Goods Reconsidered," *American Economic Review,* vol. 65 (March 1975) pp. 148–157.

The consumer decision about whether or not to keep the existing item of the product, depending on whether

$$v(t) - C_u(t) \gtrless - \frac{r_c}{1 + r_c} \min{(C_d, C_R - R)}$$

could of course be discussed for a number of special cases, such as where

$$C_u(t) = C_R = 0,$$

giving
$$v(t) \gtrless \frac{r_c R}{1 + r_c} \qquad \text{if } C_R - R < C_d$$

Of particular interest to us are the effects of the producer's policy instrument, that is, the effects of the refund offer. If we had started at a point where $R = 0$ and $C_R > C_d$, a first possible effect of an increasing R would be that the return alternative would replace the dumping alternative. A second possible effect would be that disposal would occur at an earlier date, that is, that the period during which the product is used by the consumer would be reduced. A third possible effect would be a special case of the second and would imply that the product would be returned for a refund right away.

Similarly, we may investigate the effects of stricter conditions for the right to get a refund. First, a reduction in the number of the places where returns can be made as well as stiffer requirements on the properties of the returned product eligible for a refund can be expressed as a rise in C_R. Hence the effects here would be identical to a reduction in the refund amount. Second, a restraint on the use of the refund—to products from a certain industry or a certain firm or even to one specific product only—would reduce the real value of the refund to the product owner. In principle, this could be treated as a reduction in R.

To sum up, a refund offer is here taken to affect disposal behavior if the offer reduces net disposal costs for the consumer. In this case the disposal date also may be affected and move closer. Restrictive conditions on refund rights can often be regarded as changes in individual net disposal costs, possibly influencing the choice of disposal alternative as well as disposal date.

The Purchase Decision

In this section we treat the effects of a refund offer on the purchase decision (1) when the product price remains stable and (2) when the refund offer is coupled with a price increase. We observe cases in which disposal dates and the number of units bought by the consumer are independent of the refund offer as well as cases in which they are not. (In general, the main conclusions of the following discussion can be found in the final paragraph of each subsection.)

The price may change as a consequence of the introduction of a market-generated refund system for a commodity of a given quality. As we shall see below, the price may rise or fall. From the point of view of the consumer's decision of whether or not to buy the product, the case in which the price goes up has particular interest. And because the refund offer now implies that the consumer will be confronted with the combination of a refund prospect and a price change, it is the case of a price increase that presents us with a tradeoff problem from the point of view of consumer welfare.

Assuming first that the price in fact remains unchanged, we may concentrate on the effect on consumer purchases from the refund offer alone. The reason for the refund offer may be any of those we have already discussed, such as the discovery that used products or parts can be reprocessed or reused at a profit. So an obvious effect on the consumer is that he now gets more for the same price than before the refund offer was made. This positive effect is absent only for those consumers who know they will not use the refund offer, either because they simply will not buy the product or, in case they do, because they think that alternative ways of product disposal will be preferable. Thus from the point of view of consumer welfare the introduction of a refund, *ceteris paribus,* will be a Pareto improvement, and demand for the product will not decrease.

Now, Pareto improvements and nonnegative effects on demand may no longer be the only possible results when the price goes up as an intrinsic part or as a consequence of the refund offer. Again, we need not be concerned with the exact reason for the price increase, except that we have to stress the assumption that product performance from the consumer's point of view remains the same (for example, a product remains unchanged in spite of the introduction of a return guarantee, a new container, or a more durable component that has no effect on the use or

durability of the product). If the present value of the refund for a particular consumer falls short of the price increase, the introduction of the refund will definitely result in a loss for him, assuming he buys or otherwise
would have bought this product. An overlapping group of losers are those
who know they will not use the alternative of returning the product when
they want to dispose of it. Thus we expect to have a situation in which
some consumers lose and some—those who get a net reduction in disposal costs larger than the price increase—gain and where total demand
may change in any direction.

So far we have been discussing products that may or may not be durable, where the quantity bought may or may not exceed one unit as long
as unit costs in terms of C_u, C_d, and C_R are not affected. We need to observe explicitly the case in which more than one unit may be bought by
the individual consumer and disposal costs may be endogenous. This case
will be discussed in two versions: (1) when the return has to be made, or
for other reasons actually will be made, at a given time (for example, the
"one-hoss-shay" case) and (2) when the disposal date is endogenous, as
in the preceding section. First, however, we discuss the less complicated
case in which each consumer deals with only one unit at a time (such as a
refrigerator) or a fixed number of units at a time (such as a set of tires or
batteries) and the disposal date can be treated as exogenously given.

Given number of units bought and given disposal dates. If the introduction of a return alternative does not influence the date at which the
product will be disposed of, we may treat the disposal date as given and
let the period concept be defined by the time elapsed between the purchase
date and the disposal date. This time will normally differ among consumers or product units, of course. In many cases the period will not be
long enough for interest and liquidity aspects to be important. If so, and
given our assumption that the introduction of the refund is not connected
with a change in the use value of the product, we may determine the effect
of the refund on the consumer as follows. For a consumer who knows the
size of C_R and C_d, this effect will be equal to the effect of a price reduction
in the amount of $R - C_R + C_d$, if positive, or zero otherwise. Here the net
price effect on the consumer will be $\Delta p - (R - C_R + C_d)$, or at most Δp,
where Δp is the actual price change that accompanies the introduction of
the refund.

For consumers who do not know at the time of purchase what disposal
alternative they will eventually use, because C_R or C_d is unknown, we

shall assume that behavior can be approximated by the reaction to a reduction of the expected value, $R + E(C_d - C_R)$, if positive.[4] Thus the net price effect of the refund offer for the individual consumer i is, in general,

$$\Delta p^i = \Delta p - R - E(C_d - C_R)$$

if smaller than Δp; otherwise $\Delta p^i = \Delta p$. The net effect on the individual quantity demanded will be nonnegative or nonpositive, depending on whether Δp^i is negative or positive.

When the period is long enough for interest and liquidity aspects to become important, the effect of the introduction of a refund system on the consumer may be discussed as follows. If $R + E(C_d - C_R) > 0$, the return alternative will be chosen. This will imply a reduction of the present value of disposal costs by $[R + E(C_d - C_R)] [1/(1 + r_i)]$, where r_i is the relevant discount rate for the individual. If prices change by Δp, the individual net price change will be

$$\Delta p^i = \Delta p - \frac{R + E(C_d - C_R)}{1 + r_i} \lesseqgtr 0$$

If, in addition, disposal costs would vary among individuals, some consumers might wish to keep their traditional disposal behavior, namely, when $R + E(C_d{}^i - C_R{}^i) < 0$. This group would obviously be affected by Δp alone, as Δp^i here equals $\Delta p \gtreqless 0$.

To sum up, the introduction of a refund system can be seen to affect consumer demand in this case by way of a net price change $\Delta p^i \leq \Delta p$ for individual i.

Variable number of units, variable unit disposal costs, and given disposal dates. Because several units of the commodity may be purchased by each consumer, unit disposal costs may not be constant. Assume, instead, that total disposal costs, $C_{Rtot}{}^i$ and $C_{dtot}{}^i$ are, respectively,

$$C_{Rtot}{}^i = C_R{}^i x + \bar{C}_R{}^i \quad \text{and} \quad C_{dtot}{}^i = \bar{C}_d{}^i x + \bar{C}_d{}^i$$

[4] We could assume, of course, that consumers would not be risk-neutral and that their behavior would be affected by risk aversion or any other nonneutral attitude toward risk. However, this would hardly affect the purchase decision in principle. Hence it is hardly worthwhile to use the more cumbersome exposition that an assumed risk-averse behavior would require.

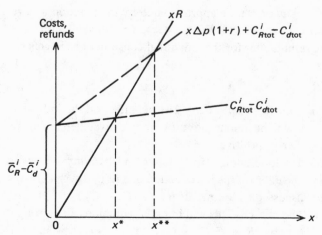

Figure 2-3.

where $\bar{C}_R{}^i$ and $\bar{C}_d{}^i$ are fixed nonnegative disposal costs and x is the quantity of the commodity. A new situation can arise if $\bar{C}_R{}^i > \bar{C}_d{}^i$. Then the choice of disposal alternative will depend also on the preferences for the commodity. As we can see in figure 2-3, where xR indicates the total gross refund value and $C_{R\text{tot}}{}^i - C_{d\text{tot}}{}^i$ the total differential disposal costs for $\bar{C}_R{}^i > \bar{C}_d{}^i$ and $C_R{}^i \lessgtr C_d{}^i$ (although $C_R{}^i > C_d{}^i$ is used for the illustration in the Figure), the pre-refund disposal alternative will be used for volumes of x below x^* and the return alternative for volumes above that volume.

Introducing a curve that portrays a version of the total addition to costs for the consumer, $x\Delta p(1 + r_i) + C_{R\text{tot}}{}^i - C_{d\text{tot}}{}^i$, we can see that for $\Delta p > 0$ and for volumes up to x^{**} the net price equivalent (Δp^i) will be positive, as the refund offer cannot compensate for all the costs involved. Above x^{**} the opposite is true, and the consumer choosing a volume above this limit may appear to have gained from the introduction of the refund system. As can be seen from figure 2-4, this is not always true. The initial "budget line" is ABC, where the distance AB is the unavoidable fixed disposal cost. The introduction of the refund system implies a new and discontinuous budget line—BD from $x = 0$ to $x = x^*$, where $\Delta p(1 + r_i) > 0$ is the total net price effect, as the traditional disposal alternative is still preferable here, and EG above $x = x^*$, where the new disposal alternative is less costly. A consumer choosing a point on the BF segment of the initial budget line may lose from the introduction of the refund system even if he ends up on the FG segment of the new budget line $(x > x^{**})$; see indifference curves I^0 and I^1. Only those who initially chose $x > x^{**}$ will be sure to gain. In addition, however, some of

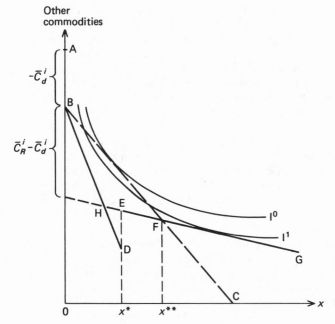

Figure 2-4.

those who initially did not consume the commodity at all (choosing point A) may now prefer to do so along the FG segment instead of remaining at point A.

A similar case in which the choice of disposal alternative depends on preferences is possible when $\bar{C}_R{}^i < \bar{C}_d{}^i$ and $C_R{}^i - C_d{}^i > R$. Here the consumer may prefer returning *small* volumes of x and using the nonreturn disposal alternative for larger volumes.

To sum up, we can interpret the effect on the consumer of the introduction of a refund system as that of a net price change $\Delta p^i \leq \Delta p$ on demand and that of a net cost decrease for disposal, when $C_R{}^i - R < C_d{}^i$, as long as marginal disposal costs equal average disposal costs. If marginal and average disposal costs deviate, the net price change may make a jump at a certain value of x at which the consumer shifts from one disposal alternative to another. Thus the choice of disposal alternative will depend on preferences as well as on the refund amount and the disposal costs. In addition, the effect on demand and on consumer welfare cannot be seen as a simple change in net prices. Moreover, as is to be expected from the introduction of a discontinuity, the stability properties of the affected market may change; not even dramatic changes in preferences may now affect demand (such as if equilibrium is at point E in figure

2-4). In other cases, however, small changes in preferences may result in substantial changes in demand (say, from the BH segment to E).

The relevance of this discontinuous case has of course to be determined by a study of empirical cost functions in each particular application. But when this case exists, a recursive analysis of the refund system, starting with a separate discussion of the disposal problem, may not be possible and hence the purchase and the disposal decisions may have to be treated as interdependent problems.

Endogenous disposal dates. The discontinuous case we have just discussed may be substantially affected when it is relevant to treat the choice of disposal dates as an endogenous variable determined by storage activities on the part of the consumer. We here, however, discuss the choice of disposal dates without explicitly observing the interdependency aspect just mentioned. As a further step toward simplification, we abstract from the case of endogenous use periods (as discussed at the end of the subsection "The Disposal Decision"); thus the commodities to be discussed here can be regarded as goods for immediate consumption.

Let us assume that the refund R per unit of the commodity is constant over time and that the storage cost r_s per period and per unit is constant regardless of the accumulated volume of the commodity. If $\bar{C}_R{}^i < \bar{C}_d{}^i$ and $C_R{}^i \leq C_d{}^i$, the return alternative will always be chosen; the optimal disposal date will depend on fixed and marginal return costs as well as on storage costs. If $\bar{C}_R{}^i < \bar{C}_d{}^i$ and $C_R{}^i > C_d{}^i$, the return alternative may still come out as cost minimal in some cases. However, because $\bar{C}_R{}^i > \bar{C}_d{}^i$ may appear to be the most common case—relevant, for example, for small-sized products that can easily be dropped in garbage cans or elsewhere—we deal with this situation in more detail here. The discussion will give an idea of the nature of the decision problem for the other cases as well.

Thus given a situation in which $\bar{C}_R{}^i > \bar{C}_d{}^i$, there may be a future date **n** at which the dumping alternative will be as expensive as the return alternative. At this date we would have

$$\sum_{t=0}^{n-1} x_t(R - C_R{}^i + C_d{}^i - r_s{}^{n-t}) = \bar{C}_R{}^i - \bar{C}_d{}^i$$

where x_t is the quantity of the commodity bought and taken out of use in period t as potentially available for disposal. This expression determines **n**, if it exists, in conjunction with the choice of an optimal x_t path. If **n** exists, the consumer cannot lose by storing all units consumed up to that date. At date **n**, it would not matter to him which of the two disposal alternatives he used if he had to get rid of his collection of used units. Since we have assumed that he does not have to do so, additional storage to $n + 1$ will be profitable for him provided that the net refund on the volume bought at date **n** will outweigh the loss of interest on the total

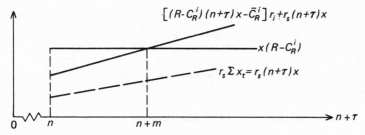

Figure 2-5.

potential refund value at date **n** and the additional storage costs; that is, it will be profitable provided that

$$x_n(R - C_R^i) - [(R - C_R^i)\sum_{t=0}^{n-1} x_t - \bar{C}_R^i]r_i - r_s\sum_{t=0}^{n-1} x_t > 0$$

where the first term is the potential net refund at date $n + 1$ for units bought at date n, the second term is the interest at individual rate r_i on potential refunds minus return costs on all other units bought so far, and the third term is the additional storage costs for units bought earlier. (This formulation disregards the interest effect of moving future rounds of disposal transactions one period farther.) Postponing returns beyond $n + 1$ will pay as long as the corresponding expression continues to be positive. An optimum date of disposal $(n + m)$ is illustrated in figure 2-5 for the case in which the consumer chooses a constant volume of $x_t = x$.

As can be seen from the case of a constant $x_t = x$ as shown in figure 2-5, the effect of increases in R and decreases in $\bar{C}_R{}^i$, $C_R{}^i$, and r_s will be, first, to increase the likelihood of there being a break-even date **n** and, second, to move **n** closer. Moreover, **m** may increase or decrease with increases in $R - C_R{}^i$, decrease with reductions in $\bar{C}_R{}^i$, and increase with reductions in r_s. Increases in $\bar{C}_d{}^i$ and $C_d{}^i$ will raise the likelihood that **n** exists and, if it does, move **n** closer without any effect on **m** (if we still assume x to be constant).

Now, the introduction of a refund system, which is our primary concern here, will affect the individual net price if **n** exists such that

$$\Delta p_t{}^i = \Delta p_t - \frac{R - C_R^i + C_d^i}{(1 + r_i)^{n+m-t}} + (n + m - t - 1)r_s \sum_{\tau=t+2}^{n+m} \frac{1}{(1 + r_i)^\tau}$$

$$t = 0, 1, \ldots, n + m - 1$$

This means that for Δp_t not increasing over time, $\Delta p_t{}^i$ will gradually diminish up to $n + m$, possibly starting from a value $\Delta p_0{}^i > \Delta p_0$. In addition, $\Delta p_t{}^i$ will be certain not to exceed Δp_t for any t only when **n** does not exist, in which case $\Delta p_t{}^i = \Delta p_t$.

Although it may appear as if the effects on consumer net prices may be considerable here, the implication of an endogenous return date is that the effects on consumer demand and welfare will be less negative or more positive than in the case of the fixed return date. The reason is, of course, that consumers are "given" additional options that, if chosen, will lead to investing in inventories to save disposal costs that in spite of increased storage costs show up as a reduction of the net price, $\Delta p_t{}^i$, and affect product demand.

THE PRODUCER DECISION

A crucial question in the case of market-generated refund systems is how the refund rate is determined and how the price of the product sold with refund rights is affected. In particular, we discuss under what conditions the price is likely to rise. Moreover, the producer may choose to make product changes, some of which may influence the use of units returned to the producer as well as the return costs for the consumer, without affecting the consumer's use of the product (for analytical convenience). This problem will be treated after we have dealt with the case of refund systems for an altogether unchanged product.

Optimal Refund Rate and Optimal Price Change

Here we discuss the case of a monopoly confronted by a linear demand function. After presenting a set of simplifying assumptions, we derive the profit-maximizing refund rate, output volume, and product price. Particular attention is given to determining the conditions (in terms of reuse values, return propensities, and demand effects) for the introduction of a refund offer that implies a price increase.

As was mentioned earlier, refund systems may be industry-wide, involving many firms, or firm-specific. When refundable items are not standardized over many producers, they may be accepted only by the producer of the original product. Two extreme cases may be distinguished here, the competitive industry with a homogeneous, standardized refund system and the single producer who has a refund system of his own and, for this or other reasons, has a monopoly position for his product. We deal with the latter case here, leaving the former case—which often would require some kind of centralized action—to be discussed along with government-initiated refund systems.

The monopoly element is obviously relevant to many real-world cases in which a refund system is introduced by an individual producer. To avoid unnecessary complications we assume (1) that there is one natural return date, possibly different for different consumers and hence that there is no endogenous service period problem or storage problem, (2) that there are no fixed disposal costs, and (3) that interest or discounting aspects are not important or can be taken into account implicitly. Moreover, we deal with a linear case in which the aggregate demand price function is given by

$$p = b - aX + eR \qquad b, a > 0, \quad 0 \le e \le 1 \qquad (2\text{-}1)$$

where p is the price of the product, X is the total quantity demanded, and $R \ge 0$ is an unconditional refund affecting quantity demanded by $(e/a)R$. The individual demand price function when no return alternative exists or when $C_R{}^i - R > C_d{}^i$ with *certainty* is

$$p = \bar{b}^i - a^i x^i - C_d{}^i = b^i - a^i x^i$$

where $b^i \equiv \bar{b}^i - C_d{}^i$. When R is introduced or raised high enough for return disposal to be chosen, to R^i for individual i, we have

$$p = b^i - a^i x^i + C_d{}^i - C_R{}^i + R = b^{*i} - a^i x^i + R$$

where $b^{*i} \equiv b^i + C_d{}^i - C_R{}^i = \bar{b}^i - C_R{}^i$ for $R > R^i$. If $R > R^i$ for all i and all relevant refund rates, the aggregate demand price function, equation (2-1), would be a simple sum of the last-mentioned individual functions making $e = 1$. But if we let R take any positive value and given that individuals have varying $C_d{}^i - C_R{}^i$ differences, a gradual shift to the return alternative can be assumed to occur when R increases. This is captured by letting e have any value (constant by assumption) between zero and one.

We deal only with interior solutions at this point, that is, $R > 0$; therefore to avoid having the producer choose $R = 0$, we assume that $C_d{}^i \le C_R{}^i$ for all i, which means that there would be no effect on demand at $R = 0$. In addition, equation (2-1) as formulated here may be used to cover the case of *uncertain* future $C_d{}^i$ and $C_R{}^i$ as well as R perceived to be uncertain by consumers. It should also be noted that e in equation (2-1) can be interpreted to reflect price discrimination between those who

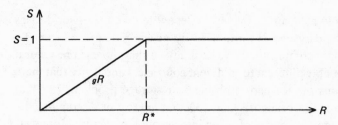

Figure 2-6.

will return used units (for whom $C_d{}^i - C_R{}^i + R > 0$) and those who will not (for whom $C_d{}^i - C_R{}^i + R < 0$).

Marginal costs of production (C_F) are assumed to be constant and equal to average costs. To begin with, we assume that C_F does not change when $R > 0$ is introduced. The gross value to the producer of returned units, V per unit before the refund is deducted, is assumed to be constant $(V \gtrless 0)$ and may be interpreted as a reuse value.

The number of units returned X_R is a fraction S of X. For simplicity, we assume S to be a linear homogeneous function of the refund; that is,

$$S = gR \qquad g > 0, \quad 0 \leq gR \leq 1$$

Thus we have

$$X_R = SX = gRX$$

At some $R = R^*$, S will equal one and hence $X_R = X$ at $R \geq R^*$ (see figure 2-6). However, as has already been pointed out, we here refrain from dealing with corner solutions and hence also those cases in which all units are returned. Thus the net total use value of returned units is given by

$$X_R(V - R) = gRX(V - R)$$

Given that the producer acts as if he knew the demand function, equation (2-1), as well as the consumers' return propensity, the profit function can be stated as

$$\Pi = pX - C_F X$$

$$= (b - aX)X - C_F X \qquad \qquad \text{for } R = 0$$

and $\Pi = (b - aX + eR)X - C_F X + gRX(V - R) \qquad \text{for } R > 0$

Maximizing profits with respect to R and X,[5] we have

$$\frac{\partial \Pi}{\partial R} = eX + gVX - 2gRX = e + gV - 2gR = 0 \qquad \text{for } X > 0$$

and

$$\frac{\partial \Pi}{\partial X} = b - 2aX + eR - C_F + gR(V - R) = 0$$

The first first-order condition determines R independently of X as

$$R = \frac{e + gV}{2g} \tag{2-2}$$

The second first-order condition—after $2gR$ has been substituted for $e + gV$ according to equation (2-2)—gives optimal output as

$$X = \frac{b - C_F + gR^2}{2a} \tag{2-3}$$

into which the optimal value of R can be inserted.

From equation (2-3) we get the effect on equilibrium output of introducing the refund system as $\Delta X = gR^2/2a$, which is positive. When equation (2-3) is inserted into the demand function, the new equilibrium price becomes

$$p_P = \frac{b + C_F}{2} + \frac{R(2e - gR)}{2}$$

With the equilibrium price prior to the introduction of R equal to

$$p_A = \frac{b + C_F}{2} \tag{2-4}$$

we have the price change,

$$\Delta p = p_P - p_A = \frac{R(2e - gR)}{2}$$

---

[5] In the guarantee case, R as seen by the producer is given either by p (money back) or by C_F (replacement value). For R to be the same for consumers and producers, we must assume the guarantee to be of the money-back kind. We deal with the guarantee case more explicitly below when we discuss product changes.

Here Δp is positive provided $R < 2e/g$ or—after we substitute for R from equation (2-2)—provided $V < 3e/g$. Given that $R > 0$ and thus $e + gV > 0$ according to equation (2-2), the provision for $\Delta p > 0$ is that $- e/g < V < 3e/g$. Cases in which $\Delta p < 0$ and $\Delta p > 0$, respectively, are illustrated in figure 2-7.

To sum up: Under the given assumptions and for $V > - e/g$, the introduction of R will increase profits and output but not always prices. In fact, increased optimal prices occur only if $3e/g > V(>-e/g)$. We should note that when e and g are strictly positive and optimal $R < V$, the producer gains from increased demand as well as from product reuse. However, owing to the demand effect e, the producer may gain even if $R > V$, that is, even if the refund is higher than the producer's reuse value of the returned product. V may even be negative, which means that the producer must pay to get rid of the returned product, without the refund system becoming unprofitable for him. But as has already been pointed out, V must be greater than $- e/g$. If, on the other hand, the demand effect is very small ($e \approx 0$), V must be positive. For $e = 0$ the optimal R is half the size of V—otherwise $R = e/2g + V/2$—in the linear case discussed here.

Other Producer Decision Variables

We also need to observe producer decisions other than the choice of refund rates, prices, and output. Here we comment briefly on some of these. (1) For what kind of purchases should the producer allow the consumer to use the refund? (2) When does it pay the producer to accept returns without offering a refund? (3) What can be said in general about the relationship between refund offers and product design? (4) What can be said more specifically about product guarantees and product design? (5) What changes of product durability may result from the introduction of a refund offer? (6) In what sense can the producer introduce a deposit in connection with a refund offer?

Ties on refund use. So far, we have not explicitly observed that there may be ties on the consumer's use of R. We would expect, of course, that e and g would be lower in the cases in which consumers get a refund only when R is to be used as partial payment for a new item bought from the producer or as complete payment in many guarantee systems, in comparison with the case in which the consumer can spend the refund as he

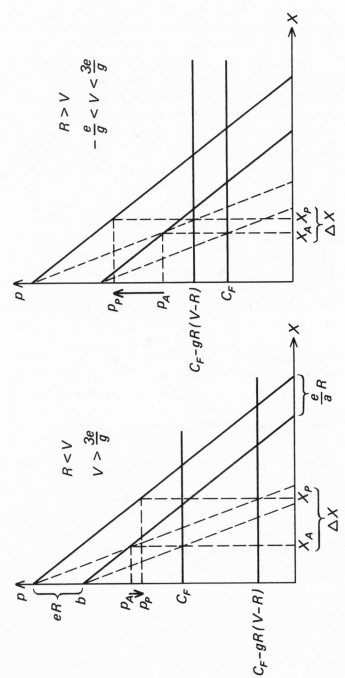

Figure 2-7.

pleases. On the other hand, ties on refund use would affect future sales by reducing the net consumer price of the product for old customers in relation to the prices of other products. This requires an extension of the analysis beyond the one-period model of the preceding subsection, which would be sufficient only as long as refunds were given in money without ties on their use. For example, this model could now refer only to the period when the refund offer was introduced, and a model like that of figures 2-1 and 2-2 could be used for subsequent periods. But given that the choice of R now has to take into account both its effect on demand now (e) and its price-discriminatory effect on future demand (as indicated in figures 2-1 and 2-2), the two models would have to be integrated. Or, for simple approximative illustrations, we could remain within the model of the preceding subsection by redefining V to include also the approximate addition to future profits from expanding the number of old customers by one.

Refunds in money and without (formal) ties in fact could have some effect on future sales, as consumers may spend a larger part of the refund on products sold by the refunding firm than they would if their income increased in other ways by the same amount. If so, the model in the preceding subsection would have to be adjusted to observe the effect on future sales regardless of the conditions for a refund.

With ties on refund use, the refund offer may be extended to certain products sold by the producer before the refund offer was introduced and even to certain products sold by others. This would promote additional increases in demand. Moreover, because the reuse values of these items may differ from those of the products now sold by the firm, we would have to differentiate between returned products with respect to V. Furthermore, because returns now could exceed sales, gR would no longer be bounded by $gR \leq 1$. This extension means also that returns will appear one round earlier than in the previous model, the unit costs being $R - V_o$ (where V_o is the reuse value of "other" products). Assuming the demand effect from this extension to be e^+R and hence the addition to units returned to be e^+R/a, we can write the profit function as

$$\Pi = (b - aX + eR + e^+R)X - C_F X + gRX(V - R) + \frac{e^+R}{a}(V_0 - R)$$

Disposal service without refunds. A special case of some importance is when the producer offers to take care of used units without paying any refund.[6] This case would be interesting if consumers otherwise would use a more expensive (possibly illegal) alternative for disposal. This system is used in some countries for medicines, paints, and other toxic remains.

Assume that this offer means that average consumer disposal costs are reduced and that $X_R = \bar{S}X$ at $R = 0$. Thus firm profits may be expressed as

$$\Pi = (b - \rho X + \bar{e})X - C_F X + \bar{S}XV \qquad (2\text{-}5)$$

Equilibrium output and price as well as ΔX and Δp can be calculated as above.

Integrating this case with that of the preceding subsection, we can express profits as

$$\Pi = (b - aX + eR + \bar{e})X - C_F X + (gR + \bar{S})X(V - R),$$

where $\bar{e}$ is strictly positive. Earlier, we took $\bar{e}$ and $\bar{S}$ to be zero, for simplicity. In the general case, optimal $R = (e + gV - \bar{S})/2g$. For optimal R to be zero, we have $\bar{S} \geq e + gV$, with V bounded from below for a return disposal to be at all profitable for the producer.

Changes in product quality. So far we have discussed decision variables—price, refund rate, refund conditions, and disposal service without a formal refund—that do not involve any product change. The introduction of a refund system may, of course, open up a multitude of alternatives having to do with changes in product quality. In the present context we cannot discuss quality changes that turn the product into an entirely new one; we can discuss only changes that do not affect the consumer's use of the product. Other changes would make a comparison with the situation prior to the introduction of the refund system impossible. However, quality changes that affect only the "returnability" of the product or the producer's use of the returned product may be quite important.

In fact, it may be that no return-refund system can be introduced without at least some product change, and this change may involve additions to production costs. As one extreme, the product may have been such that there simply was not anything to return. In such a case, when a return

6 This is one corner solution ($R = 0$) that the model in the preceding section was not designed to take care of.

system with a refund instrument is considered as a possible way of increasing profits, a product change must be made in order for such plans to materialize.

In other cases it may be profitable, though not necessary, to make product changes in connection with the introduction of a refund system. For example, product changes may make it less expensive for the consumer to return the product, by reducing C_R. Here the producer could get an increase in the demand effect e and return propensity g in exchange for an increase in C_F. Or the value V of the returned product may be increased by changing the product design. Thus, in general, an increase in e and g or in V or in all three can be achieved by adding to the production cost C_F.

It must be observed, however, that when $R > V$ profits will increase with a *reduction* in g. A change in product quality that reduces g may be achieved in some cases at a lower level of production cost C_F and in others at a higher level. The reason is that while increased returnability of a product can be expected to make the product more expensive, say by adding a new characteristic to it, reduced returnability may not always lead to lower costs. In fact, it may require that more costly characteristics deterring returns are added to the product. In particular, in cases where a reduction in returnability—a lower g—can be achieved at a lower C_F, the optimum quality change may be one in which g as well as V and e are smaller. If so, the profit-maximizing move would be to introduce a refund system while the product is being changed, so that the use of the refund option is reduced, thereby lowering the demand effect e, the return propensity g, and possibly also the value of returns V.[7]

Product guarantees. Refund systems in the form of product guarantees may be particularly likely to give rise to product changes and increased costs. As was indicated earlier, R may no longer be viewed as a separate parameter in such systems. In a money-back guarantee, R would equal price, and in a free-replacement guarantee, R from the producer's point of view would equal C_F. If we think of a product change here as one that reduces the probability that the product will break down in a prespecified fashion during a given period of time, the producer could "buy" a reduction in the number of returns by increasing product quality and, normally,

---

[7] Reducing g will in itself affect the optimal refund. From equation (2-2) we have $\partial R / \partial g = -e/2g^2$ and hence the optimal R would be larger whenever the optimal product change is one that reduces g.

production costs. In this case, he is, of course, never interested in increasing the number of returns, as R in both guarantee systems will exceed V, the value of the returned malfunctioning unit.

Formally, we may write the profit function in the guarantee case as

$$\Pi = (b - aX + e_G)X - C_F X + S_G X(V - R)$$

where e_G is the positive demand effect of a given guarantee system (e_G being different in free-replacement and money-back guarantees), S_G is the fraction of the products returned and a decreasing function of C_F, and V and e_G are assumed to be independent of C_F.

Maximizing Π with respect to X, we get X_P, the optimal output after the guarantee is introduced, as

$$X_P = \frac{b - C_F}{2a} + \frac{e_G}{2a} + \frac{S_G(V - C_F)}{2a} \qquad \text{for } R = C_F$$

(for free-replacement guarantees) and

$$X_P = \frac{b - C_F}{2a} + \frac{e_G}{2a} + \frac{S_G(V - C_F)}{2a(1 - S_G)} \qquad \text{for } R = p_P$$

(for money-back guarantees), where $X_P \gtrless X_A$ (optimal output prior to the introduction of the guarantee). Inserting X in the demand function, we get

$$p_P = \frac{b + C_F}{2} + \frac{e_G}{2} + \frac{S_G(C_F - V)}{2} \qquad \text{for } R = C_F$$

and

$$p_P = \frac{b + C_F}{2} + \frac{e_G}{2} + \frac{S_G(C_F - V)}{2(1 - S_G)} \qquad \text{for } R = p_P$$

both of which are larger than P_A in equation (2-4), as $S_G \leqslant 1$ and $C_F > V$ (the value of the returned deficient product being less for the producer than the costs of a new product). In other words, prices are certain to rise in our linear model as a consequence of the introduction of a guarantee system.

Now, maximizing with respect to C_F, we get

$$\frac{\partial \Pi}{\partial C_F} = -X + \frac{dS_G}{dC_F} X(V - C_F) - S_G X = 0 \qquad \text{for } R = C_F \qquad \text{(2-6)}$$

and

$$\frac{\partial \Pi}{\partial C_F} = -X + \frac{dS_G}{dC_F} X(V - p_P) - S_G X \frac{dp_P}{dC_F} = 0 \quad \text{for } R = p_P \quad (2\text{-}7)$$

Here we recall that dS_G/dC_F has been assumed to be negative and that V is smaller than both C_F and p_P. Equation (2-6) can be rewritten as

$$\frac{dS_G}{dC_F} (V - C_F) = S_G + 1 \quad (2\text{-}6')$$

which determines the optimum value of C_F for $R = C_F$. As

$$\frac{dp_P}{dC_F} = \frac{1}{2(1 - S_G)} > 0$$

equation (2-7) turns into

$$\frac{dS_G}{dC_F} (V - p_P) = \frac{S_G}{2(1 - S_G)} + 1 \quad (2\text{-}7')$$

For the initially given C_F, the left-hand side in equation (2-7') is larger than that in equation (2-6'), as p_P always exceeds C_F. Similarly, for the given C_F, the right-hand side in equation (2-7') is smaller than that in equation (2-6') as long as $S_G < 1/2$, which is reasonable to assume. Thus we conclude that in order to meet the optimum conditions of equations (2-6') and (2-7'), more will be spent on product change for $R = p_P$ than for $R = C_F$. This is based on the assumption that the function $S_G(C_F)$ is the same in both systems.

We have here dealt with increases in reliability or durability in the sense of a reduction in the probability that a product will break down during a given period. However, we also need to observe the possible incentives for changing durability in the sense of making the "normal" product last longer. We now turn to discuss this aspect of quality change.

Product durability. Refund systems may have a positive influence on product durability. However, as we discussed in the subsection "The Disposal Decision," the period for which the consumer will use a particular durable good of given quality may be shortened by the introduction of a refund. Thus durability in this sense would be reduced. The consequent increase in future demand—moving replacements closer in time—may be one reason why V (as redefined on page 34) is positive and hence why a refund is offered.

Our present interest, however, is in the effects on product design: will the introduction of refunds make it profitable for the producer to change the physical properties of the product so that its durability, *ceteris paribus,* will change? To deal with this issue in more detail—keeping in mind that durability has important consequences, such as for the volume of wastes— we assume that in the pre-refund situation durability is optimal from the producer's point of view. In other words, we assume that a marginal change in product durability L that affects demand today ($db/dL > 0$) and costs today ($dC_F/dL > 0$) and that delays future profits from replacement sales ($-\Delta\Pi_f$) leaves the present value of total profits unchanged; that is,

$$\frac{db}{dL} X_A - \frac{dC_F}{dL} X_A - \Delta\Pi_f = 0$$

We assume db/dL and dC_F/dL to be constant. Moreover, we assume that in the post-refund situation there is no call for change of product design in any respect other than durability. Finally, we assume that $-\Delta\Pi_f$, the effect of a change in durability on the present value of future profits, is not affected by the institutional change in itself.[8] Then, given that the introduction of a refund system for today's output will increase optimal output ($X_P > X_A$), the effect on the present value of total profits is

$$\frac{db}{dL} X_P - \frac{dC_F}{dL} X_P - \Delta\Pi_f > 0$$

that is, that profits would increase by an increase in product durability.

We must now, however, take into account that changes in product durability design change the time at which the products will be returned to the producers for a refund. Although we repressed the time dimension in the profit function discussed above, we may regard the effect on product returns of a product quality change toward greater durability as an interest gain of postponing net refund payouts, $R - V$. If we let the period concept

---

[8] To be specific, Π_f are expected future *maximum* profits, which may or may not require a *future* refund system. In other words, the issue here is whether or not to introduce a refund offer for sales today. Thus the change in future profits ($-\Delta\Pi_f$) considered here refers only to the delay in replacement sales.

here be defined by the resulting change in durability and r be the relevant interest rate, the interest gain will be

$$-gRX_P \frac{r(V-R)}{(1+r)^t}$$

Thus when a refund system is introduced, the total effect of product durability change becomes

$$\left(\frac{db}{dL} - \frac{dC_F}{dL}\right) X_P - gRX_P \frac{r(V-R)}{(1+r)^t} - \Delta\Pi_f$$

If $R < V$, the implication is that each unit returned will yield a net addition to profits and thus that there will be an interest loss from producing a more durable product, and so it may pay the firm to reduce L. But when $R > V$, we are certain, given the assumptions, that the total effect of increasing L is positive and thus that the introduction of the refund system makes it worthwhile to make the product more durable.

The deposit aspect. Particularly since the introduction of a refund system may make it profitable and sometimes necessary to alter the product so that it becomes more expensive (in the sense of increasing production costs, *ceteris paribus*), we must consider the deposit aspect of the refund system. Although it is somewhat arbitrary to talk about a deposit in a market-generated refund system—one may always call a part of the price a deposit once there is a refund offer regardless of whether or not prices or product durability is reduced in the process—it may be natural for producers to start using the deposit concept when products are made more durable or when prices go up ($\Delta p > 0$), or both. In fact, splitting the amount that the consumer has to pay into two components, a price and a deposit, would probably be a part of the marketing strategy of a profit-maximizing producer. But it should also be noted that this formal labeling may be an efficient instrument for informing consumers about the existing refund option.

Whereas in the case of market-generated refund systems a distinction between deposits and prices is more or less arbitrary, deposits will be seen to play a more prominent role when we discuss government intervention in such systems and analyze government-initiated refund systems in the next chapter.

SUMMARY

In addition to capturing a reuse value of products or parts returned to the producer, possible motives for producer-initiated refund systems are that refund offers may allow the firm to increase profits by price discrimination, by speeding up the consumers' replacement purchases, or simply by making the products more attractive to a sufficient number of consumers and hence stimulating demand.

From the consumer's point of view a refund offer, other than a product guarantee, may affect nothing but his disposal decision, in that he returns the product instead of using other forms of disposal (such as dumping) and that he may dispose of it earlier. But as was just stated, there may be effects on the demand for the product as well. These effects are then determined by the (expected) impact on consumer disposal costs—or by the insurance value attached to a product guarantee—as well as by the price change ($\gtrless 0$) accompanying the refund offer. If the price goes up, certain consumers may lose, in particular those whose disposal decisions remain unchanged or those who attach a low value to product guarantees. Whereas product guarantees have been shown to increase prices in the linear case analyzed here, price increases for profitable refund systems in general are likely to occur only under certain conditions with small or negative reuse values for the product or with large effects on demand, or both.

We have seen in the case discussed here that the profit-maximizing refund rate can be determined independently of the equilibrium price (or output) decision. As a special case the optimal refund rate may be zero, the implication being simply that the producer provides a facility for return disposal. Aside from determining optimal prices, outputs, and refund rates, the producer can, as we have shown, choose among various sets of conditions for accepting returns.

We have also seen that the prospect of a profitable refund system can be expected to provide incentives for product quality change, such as changes in product durability. However, all such changes do not necessarily imply a more expensive product quality or a higher rate of product returns.

3 GOVERNMENT-INITIATED DEPOSIT–REFUND SYSTEMS
The Case of Consumer-Paid Deposits

INTRODUCTION

So far we have dealt with producer-initiated deposit–refund systems and their direct effects on producers and consumers. Because such systems may have effects outside the market of the product involved, we need to broaden the analysis to take these effects into account. Market-borne indirect effects are of minor interest here. Thus we do not explicitly deal with the effects of deposit–refund systems on secondhand markets for the refundable product (where we can expect prices to be affected), on markets for scrapped products (where the supply may change), or on markets for inputs to the producer of the refundable product (where demand may be affected). Instead, we focus on the nonmarket effects of deposit–refund systems, such as effects on the dumping of used products and on the waste volume.

The fact that third-party effects and, in particular, third-party external effects are involved may present a case for government intervention both in markets where producer-initiated deposit–refund systems are in operation and in markets where firms have not found it profitable to introduce them. However, the role of government with respect to deposit–refund systems is not limited to the efficiency (and possibly distributional) aspects of these third-party effects. Market prices may deviate from social optimal prices for other reasons as well, and deposit–refund systems may be one way to achieve the required adjustment in resource allocation. In this section we present a general background on government-initiated deposit–refund systems and a brief overview of different possible motives for using them.

Such a system may be used, for example, when market prices for exhaustible resources are judged to be too low because of an underestimation of future demand or an overestimation of future supply and when direct measures to increase these prices are ruled out. Here a government-initiated deposit–refund system can help by promoting reuse and recycling of primary products and hence reducing present demand for virgin primary products. Moreover, a temporary inflexibility in waste disposal habits may exist that "correct" long-run resource prices cannot overcome but that a deposit–refund system could remove. Or an inflexibility may exist because of indivisibilities such that small volumes of reuse or recycling are not profitable, and hence these activities cannot get started. Or the government may simply have a merit want with respect to conservation. In the last two cases, deposit–refund systems may prove to be efficient incentive-reinforcing or incentive-creating policy instruments.

The producer-initiated deposit–refund systems discussed in the preceding chapter may, of course, refer to producer goods as well as consumer goods, which are our primary concern here. In fact, many existing market-generated deposit–refund systems refer to transactions among producers only (such as wholesale containers). However, producer-paid deposits may be called for in other instances as well. If consumers of a certain commodity or in a specific area were to unite, it might well be that additional "market-generated" deposit–refund systems would emerge. In particular, consumers could benefit from certain long-term commitments by producers regarding, for example, restoration of plant lots and open pit mines after the operation is shut down, availability of spare parts for durable goods subject to model change, protection against hazardous products or malfunctioning products, and protection against producer bankruptcy affecting ongoing undertakings such as construction work and charter flight packages in which consumers would be seriously hurt by halfway fulfillment of contracts. In such cases, government may act in the place of consumers by forcing producers to pay deposits (or post bonds) as a guarantee for consumer protection.[1] In other instances, producers may

---

[1] As we can see from the examples given here, a producer guarantee can be viewed as a (deposit) refund system offered to consumers as we did in the preceding chap-

buy time by making government-required deposits pending a government decision with respect to the production or sales of a product that the producers allege meets certain legal standards. Such government decisions can be time-consuming because extensive firm-independent research or intricate legal procedures may be required or simply because there may be bottlenecks in the testing process.

Thus government may have reasons for introducing deposit–refund systems or intervening in those already initiated by producers in a number of different market situations, if alternative policy measures prove to be less appropriate or are legally banned. In addition, however, the legislative branch of government may consider different ways of improving efficiency in the administrative branch, and deposit–refund systems may in some cases play a role here as well. For example, delayed action by government agencies or local governments handling permits of various kinds or deciding on public projects may impose substantial costs on individuals and firms. In such cases the burden could be shifted at least partly to the agency or local government to speed up the administrative process and to provide incentives for new and improved handling routines. Standards imposed by the legislature in these areas can under certain conditions be combined with economic incentives in the form of deposit–refund systems (refunds given when the standards are met) or fines on substandard handling (which might amount to the same thing in this case).

In what follows, we treat separately the cases of consumer-paid, producer-paid, and government-paid deposits. In all these cases, we assume that (central) government—directly or indirectly—collects the deposits and finances the refund payments. In this chapter we focus on the first case and discuss optimal government management of consumer-paid deposit systems and some general arguments for adopting this instrument instead of others in the pursuit of a given set of government policy goals.

In the next section we state the assumed policy objectives of the government and indicate potential areas where consumer-paid deposit systems can be used. The problem of optimal deposits (optimal prior to a comparison with alternative instruments) is analyzed in the section after that, where we also try to identify the main effects on different groups of economic agents. In a third section, deposit–refund systems are compared with alternative policy systems.

---

ter. In addition, a producer guarantee can be imposed on producers or its validity secured via deposit–refund systems imposed on producers by a government acting in the consumers' interest.

CONSUMER-PAID DEPOSITS
AND POLICY OBJECTIVES

The deposit or "tax" part of a deposit–refund system finances the refund or subsidy part. Hence it neutralizes the effect on money income for those agents who choose to meet the requirements for a refund. Others lose money income by not qualifying for a refund; for these agents the overall effect of the deposit–refund system will be that of a charge on a certain kind of behavior. A simple charge, that is, one that is not preceded by a deposit payment, acts as a push incentive, an incentive to move away from "undesirable" behavior, whereas a refund option acts as a pull incentive, an incentive to move toward "good" behavior.

Now, what is to be regarded as "undesirable" or "good" is given here by a set of government policy objectives. This set, we assume, consists of social efficiency, based on consumer preferences (with exceptions), and certain policy constraints of a legal nature or of some other origin, such as lack of information or prejudice. In general, we do not try to explain why such constraints exist; we simply accept them. However, the basis for the existence of constraints should be made somewhat more explicit in one respect, and that is when the basis is given by a set of political valuations regarding the distribution of real income. It is assumed here that the implication of "distributive constraints" is that the real income of certain consumers (such as those in low-income households) is not allowed to deteriorate—at all or in particular dimensions—as a consequence of a particular policy choice. The reason deposit–refund systems may be interesting in this perspective was indicated in chapter 1: a deposit–refund device has a built-in potential for protecting consumers against money income losses from policy measures.

From an analytical viewpoint we can identify possible uses of consumer-paid deposit–refund systems for policy purposes in areas where there are externalities (including intergenerational externalities) and discontinuities in supply or demand (such as those resulting from economies of scale or inertia in consumer response). More specifically, we can distinguish four important categories of cases in which deposit–refund systems may be used.

First, detrimental external effects from pollution (such as from the dumping of oil and chemicals in the environment) and from littering (such as leaving containers, tires, and hulks in conspicuous places) may be reduced by requiring deposits on the products when bought and establishing a right to refunds if the products are returned to specific points

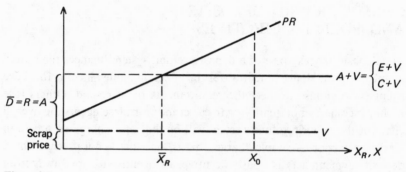

Figure 3-1.

where the detrimental effects are less pronounced or nonexistent. In some cases, this could also reduce waste management costs in comparison with the costs of the alternative, dumping the products in the municipal waste stream. Thus the detrimental external effect avoided and the extra waste management cost avoided by turning the product over to a reception unit would be relevant for determining the deposit–refund rate. In some cases, however, the alternative to having the product returned might be that the dumped product is taken care of by a mobile collection unit. If so, the relevant value of returning the product would be the collection cost avoided, that is, the costs of identification, legal processing, collection, and transportation as well as possible external effects up to the point of removal. In an otherwise efficient economy, we could assume that the relevant value actually would be the lowest of the two, as the solution corresponding to that value would be the one preferred by the government.

In figure 3-1, A is either the value of the external effect avoided E or the net collection cost avoided C, whichever is the relevant alternative. V is the maximum reuse value or the zero-profit market scrap price ($V \gtrless 0$), and PR is the consumers' propensity to return used products of a given type. The PR curve shows the supply of returned products in the order of an increasing supply price (possibly identical to the cost difference of return disposal over the alternative form of disposal). Thus supply is assumed to increase with the refund R ($R = D$, the deposit). A and V are taken to be constant in the interesting interval or at least not increasing with the volume of returned products (X_R) more than PR does.

Given that the PR curve can be taken to reveal the social marginal cost of products returned and that the social marginal benefit is given by $A +$

V, the optimal deposit rate is $\bar{D} = A$. Thus, in all, the consumer would be paid $R + V$ for a product return: $R = \bar{D} = A$ as a refund and V as a scrap or reuse price. If the optimal volume returned $(\bar{X}_R)$ fell short of the total volume of products disposed of (X_0), $X_0 - \bar{X}_R$ would be the optimal volume of wastes or pollution under the deposit–refund system. Because the PR curve lacks any meaning beyond X_0, a smaller X_0 would eventually make $\bar{X}_R = X_0$ and reduce the optimal deposit below $\bar{D}$. (The effect of the deposit–refund system on product demand is omitted here, but will be discussed in the next section.)

Second, in an economy in which for political reasons the price of a primary product is kept at a level below the present value of future use, an adverse external effect on future generations may arise. If, however, the present volume of extraction were regulated to a level corresponding to that which an equilibrium price equal to the present value of future use would have brought about, the burden of the inflexible price, that is, of the rationing required, would be on the present generation instead. In either of these two cases, the government may feel free to intervene in existing markets (or open up new ones) for reuse or recycling of used commodities containing the primary product in question. This intervention may, for example, concern any kind of metal, or it may concern oil used for lubrication; it may concern a metal like aluminum because it requires less energy when produced from scrap than from bauxite. When a deposit–refund system is used in such a case, the deposit could be attached to the input of the primary product in the manufacturing of certain products and levied when the manufactured product is produced and sold to consumers. The refund again determines the volume returned to a point of reception for reuse or recycling. And if the net value of the returned product is equal to $A + V$ at the reception unit, the partial analysis of the optimal deposit–refund system can be cast as in figure 3-1. However, this net value, and hence the refund payment, has to be determined either on the basis of the present value of future use of the primary product or, in the rationing case mentioned, on the basis of the shadow price of the volume allowed to be sold. As the rationing case was presented, these two estimates should coincide.

Third, we may have a situation in which used products containing a certain raw material could be reprocessed at a long-term equilibrium scrap price that would guarantee both a large volume of voluntary or "automatic" returns and a profitable reprocessing activity. However, the fact that such a market solution can be assumed to exist may not consti-

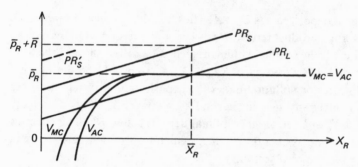

Figure 3-2.

tute a strong enough incentive for this solution to materialize. Increasing returns to scale in production, transportation, and so on,[2] and a slow adjustment of the supply of used products to the new type of disposal may make the length of the transition period uncertain and short-term losses considerable. Thus the combination of a decreasing-cost structure and low flexibility in the supply of material to the reprocessing industry may stop private firms from starting up markets of this kind. A government with another attitude to risk (say, risk neutrality) or with another set of instruments at its disposal than a private firm would have (say, a right or an ability to enforce a system of deposits on several uses of a given material) may find it advantageous to help start up, and possibly operate in, such markets.[3]

The situation may be described as in figure 3-2, where PR_L and PR_S are the long-term and short-term propensities to return used products, respectively, and where V_{AC} and V_{MC} are the reuse values net of average and marginal reprocessing costs, respectively. The price of the reprocessing output, such as a secondary metal, is assumed to be given. In the long run,

[2] This has been relevant, for example, for recycling beverage containers as well as tires. See Organization for Economic Cooperation and Development (OECD), *Beverage Containers—Reuse or Recycling* (Paris, 1978) p. 137 and the following footnote.

[3] A case in point may be the project of producing carbon black from scrapped tires in Scandinavia. It has been suggested that one such plant would be efficient for the whole Scandinavian market. It would require, however, that a substantial number of the tires now being scrapped in all the Scandinavian countries be made available to this plant for it to reach a profitable output level. Given that these plans and predictions remain accurate when scrap tires are priced at their opportunity cost level, a temporary refund may be an appropriate action for the Scandinavian governments to undertake to make this project materialize.

equilibrium scrap prices equal to $\bar{p}_R$ are sufficient to get a return quantity $\bar{X}_R$, which in turn will yield a total net value high enough to pay $\bar{p}_R\bar{X}_R$. However, to establish the market, higher scrap prices are needed, say, to $\bar{p}_R + \bar{R}$, in order to get the same volume of used products for reprocessing. As before, $\bar{p}_R + \bar{R}$ is the total payment per unit for these products, $P_R = V$ is the market reuse value, and $\bar{R}$ is the refund. (Of course, $\bar{X}_R$ may not be the optimal volume for both the long-run and the short-run equilibrium with a deposit–refund system.)

We may add that although economies of scale in the reprocessing industry make the case discussed now more likely, they are not necessary for this case to occur. If $V_{AC} = V_{MC}$ for all X_R and if PR_S were smaller (see PR'_S in figure 3-2) while PR_L were as before, the problem would arise again. The potential relevance of this problem may be considerable. Given the habits of consumers, say, to dump used products of a certain kind, the appearance of a scrap price or refund at a low level ($\bar{p}_R$) sufficient to make the return alternative the least expensive might not provide a strong enough incentive to change these habits; on the other hand, if consumers were used to returning used products, prices at this level would be sufficient for sustaining a reprocessing market. Expressed in another way, there may be a one-time information and adjustment cost for consumers to change their disposal behavior. If so, the argument for government intervention to reinforce incentives through a deposit–refund system so that the change actually occurs presupposes that these one-time costs are not substantial enough to keep the change from being socially efficient. A thorough analysis of this case would require an investigation into the minimum adjustment time to a deposit–refund system and whether in fact such a system can and will be withdrawn once it has been introduced (and consumers have become used to it).

Fourth, the government may look at recycling as a merit want in the sense of being an explicit deviation from consumer preferences (that is, not based on differences in information or planning capacity between government and the individual consumer). Here the government may be viewed as attaching a higher price to recycled products than the market does (at p_R) or as attaching a lower consumer cost of returning used products than consumers themselves do. The latter formulation can be directly applied to figure 3-2, with PR_S now interpreted as the (short-run and long-run) supply curve of consumer returns and PR_L as the government merit want version of this supply. The government could implement its version of the optimum by introducing a deposit–refund system with a refund equal to the difference between PR_S and PR_L. Given this particular policy goal, the economic problem is to find the most efficient way of attaining it. And in that context as well, we would be interested in the effects and specific merits of a deposit–refund system.

We have now mentioned four categories of consumer-paid deposits that a government may find appropriate to introduce. We could have also included a government-initiated product warranty system. In fact, this additional category may be particularly relevant, since a deficiency in market-generated guarantee systems may be attributed to inflexibility or merit want problems similar to those we just discussed. As a possible example, product guarantees in the form of a "cooling-off" period during which consumers have the right to return the product without any particular reason are rarely generated by the market economy. Still, such guarantees, as well as those of a more conventional type, may benefit a few people a great deal, sufficiently to make the government force this institutional change on those consumers who believe they would lose from the resulting price increase or compulsory insurance premium.[4] We refrain, however, from dealing with the guarantee case at this point and return to it in conjunction with producer-paid deposits in the next chapter.

To facilitate the analysis of the effects of consumer-paid deposit–refund systems, we integrate the four cases into one common exposition. In general, we avoid paying explicit attention to the fact that part of the payments for returned products consists of a market net reuse value ($\gtrless 0$). Thus we assume this value to be zero, except when its magnitude is crucial for the analysis. That is to say, a refund equal to the deposit is what the consumer gets when he returns the product, and the refund may now reflect external effects avoided, a shadow price of scarce exhaustible resources, or reinforcement of incentives optimal in a long-run perspective or merit want valuations, and so on. Moreover, we suppress the particular case in which there are decreasing costs in the reception, collection, reprocessing, and recycling industry and view the deposit–refund system essentially as illustrated in figure 3-3. Against this background, we now turn to the specific effects of a deposit–refund system, such as the effects

[4] A complete set of contingent commodity markets in a perfect market economy could have eliminated this possible need for government intervention. Consumers would have been able to buy protection against exogenously determined product failure to the extent desired by each individual. As is well known, transaction costs prevent the market economy from establishing such a complete set of markets; and the few contingent commodity markets established by the market may not be an efficient selection.

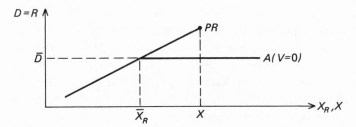

Figure 3-3.

on the behavior of the agents and the markets involved, the prices, the product design, the effect of a surplus of deposits over refunds, and the interest on deposits.

THE EFFECTS OF CONSUMER-PAID DEPOSITS

What we have just said implies that we do not deal with government-initiated deposit–refund systems as a simple extension of the refund system discussed in the preceding chapter. Such a system could exist, of course, when the government required certain firms to accept product returns at a refund. (This is essentially what actual legislation of mandatory deposits on beverage containers in certain parts of the United States amounts to.) Firms selling the products may then use the notion of a deposit in the amount of the refund or may be required to do so by law. But, as was pointed out earlier, this kind of deposit will not prevent the system from being just a refund system. We do not deal with this alternative (simple refund systems imposed by government) because it cannot be expected to work properly at refund levels above the net reuse value. If R was required to exceed V, firms would lose from each unit returned (although they might benefit from increased demand due to the return-refund offer). Hence the individual firm in a market with many firms or with no or insufficient positive demand effects could be expected to discourage returns, say, by increasing return costs for consumers directly or indirectly.[5] This is all the more troublesome because optimal

[5] A return cost increase could arise even if firms were required by law to accept returns. For example, firms may successfully try to convince the regulating authorities that high collection costs make it too expensive for them to collect used items except for a fee or that consumers should deliver the products to a special (distant) collection station.

total payments for the returned product should exceed V in the cases mentioned above. That is to say, to create correct incentives for product returns, consumers should receive V plus a refund equal to A in the general case of figure 3-3 (where we had $V = 0$ for convenience). In such cases, therefore, deposits would have to be paid to the government (indirectly), with refunds paid by the government (indirectly) to avoid having the system obstructed by the market.

Thus we assume here that the government-initiated deposit paid by the consumer of a product is transferred to the government or that the system is administered in a way that has the same effect. The refunds paid when the used products are returned in a specified manner to a specified place are drawn from this government fund of deposits. Interest aspects and the operational problems connected with long-term deposits are left aside for the time being.

Demand

The effect on demand for the product on which there is now a deposit to be paid depends, as before, on the available disposal alternatives. Given that unit costs of return $(C_R{}^i)$ and unit costs of alternative disposal $(C_d{}^i)$ are constant for each individual consumer, demand will tend to increase if $C_R{}^i < C_d{}^i$. In other words, the introduction of the deposit–refund system means that the consumer simply gets a new and cheaper way to get rid of his used products. Because he will return the products whatever the deposit–refund rate is, this rate is irrelevant to him (aside from the interest, liquidity, and other such aspects that we have left out here). If $C_R{}^i < C_d{}^i$ for all consumers, there would be a tendency for aggregate demand to increase. Moreover, given that certain administrative costs could be avoided at $D = 0$, as compared to $D > 0$, optimal deposits would be zero here (see the PR^1 curve in figure 3-4).

Now, if $C_R{}^i > C_d{}^i$ for an individual consumer, his demand would tend to decrease for $D > 0$, as he would now have to use a more expensive disposal alternative or abstain from the refund. In fact, he will abstain from the refund by choosing the dumping alternative and take the corresponding loss, *ceteris paribus,* as long as $R = D < D^* \equiv C_R{}^i - C_d{}^i$. The loss will equal D and will increase as D increases up to $D = D^*$. At refunds above D^*, the consumer will use the return alternative, and his loss will remain at D^* per unit of the product. Thus demand will tend to decrease with D up to D^* and then remain unaffected. If all consumers had the same disposal costs or at least the same disposal cost difference

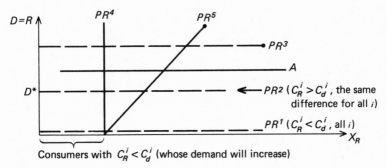

Figure 3-4.

$(C_R{}^i - C_d{}^i)$, aggregate demand would decrease, and the optimal deposit would be D^*, if D^* is less than the social value of returns A (see PR^2 in figure 3-4). If D^* exceeded A, we would have $D = 0$ and no return alternative (see PR^3).

When $C_R{}^i - C_d{}^i$ is positive but differs among consumers, $D_i{}^*$ would also differ. Hence aggregate demand will vary inversely with D and the propensity to use the return alternative will increase with D. The length (related to total consumption or total stocks of X) and the steepness of the PR curve will depend on individual cost differences as well as on the price elasticity of demand (D being the price equivalent Δp^i for each individual up to $D_i{}^*$). If all consumers with $C_R{}^i > C_d{}^i$ had an infinitely elastic demand above the product price given so far, they would drop out as soon as $D > 0$, giving a PR curve like PR^4 in figure 3-4. Except for this extreme case, we would have a curve like PR^5, although discontinuities in the frequency distribution of consumers on $C_R{}^i - C_d{}^i$ levels are likely to exist and, if so, would introduce vertical and horizontal portions of this curve.

We took a PR curve like PR^5 to be our general case above. Here the optimal D, in fact, would equal A, with part of the products bought being returned, unless PR^5 stops short of that level. (If it does, the minimum optimal D would be correspondingly smaller, and all products would be returned.) And in this general case, the net effect on aggregate demand of the deposit–refund system will depend on (1) the demand increase from a reduction in the price equivalent for consumers with $C_R{}^i < C_d{}^i$, (2) the elasticity of demand with respect to the price equivalent, which increases with D for consumers with $C_R{}^i > C_d{}^i$, and (3) the social value of the products returned A. The lower A and $C_R{}^i$ are, *ceteris paribus,* the higher is the probability that the net aggregate demand effect is positive.

Prices and Production

If the product is produced by a *monopolist* (the case discussed in the preceding chapter but now with $V = 0$), the effect on profits of a government-initiated deposit system may be derived from the profit function,

$$\text{II} = (b - aX + \bar{e} - e'R)X - C_F X \tag{3-1}$$

Here $\bar{e}$ is the positive effect on demand price at $R = D = 0$ (from consumers with $C_R{}^i < C_d{}^i$), and $-e'$ is the marginal negative effect on demand price at $R = D > 0$ (from consumers with $C_R{}^i > C_d{}^i$).[6] The latter effect is of course negative now (compare the positive effect of R in a pure refund system in equation (2-1)) because R is balanced by D for those who have $0 < C_R{}^i - C_d{}^i < R$ and D is a net cost for those who have $C_R{}^i - C_d{}^i \geq R$, which makes product disposal more expensive for all in these two subgroups. The profit-maximizing price and output will go up if $\bar{e} - e'R > 0$ for an optimal $R = D \leq A$ and will fall if $\bar{e} - e'R < 0$.

If the product is produced by an industry under *perfect competition,* the demand price function will of course be affected by the deposit as in the monopoly case (see the expression within parentheses in equation (3-1)). Moreover, equilibrium price and output would change in the directions indicated in the monopoly case. The difference between the two cases is the usual one—a reduction in net demand leads to profit losses (and, possibly, a shutdown) in the monopoly case and to a reduction in the number of firms in the perfectly competitive case.

The less evident and analytically more complicated effects of the deposit–refund system arise from the incentives to adjust the design of the product. There do not seem to be any particular incentives to change the durability of the product, as the product returns constitute a separate issue and no longer are a built-in producers' interest as in the market-generated case. But there are certainly incentives to change product quality in other respects. First, the presence of a deposit system makes it worthwhile to change product quality, so that $C_R{}^i$ is reduced unless identical changes would occur in $C_d{}^i$. In other words, the monopoly or the emerging (temporary) monopolistic competitor in the otherwise perfectly competitive industry may trade a higher C_F for an increase in demand from a reduction in $C_R{}^i$ affecting all consumers except those who still have $C_R{}^i - C_d{}^i \geq R$.

---

[6] To repeat, II is the monopolist's profits, X the aggregate product volume, and C_F the marginal costs of production, equal to average costs.

Second, there may be far-reaching effects on the input structure of the product in cases in which the deposit–refund system refers only to a part of the commodity. For example, it might now pay the producer to accept a certain increase in C_F in order to reduce the content of a polluting agent or a primary input, provided deposits per product unit and hence expected negative effects on demand were reduced accordingly. An exception might arise when there is a reduction in the net reuse value as a consequence of the product change in the "incentive reinforcement" case and the government still finds it optimal not to change the return incentives and thus the total payments per unit; here the government would have to increase the deposit rate, hence neutralizing (some of) the effects of the product. Otherwise, a reduction in optimal return payments would arise, which, if it were to affect actual payments, would lead to an increase in aggregate demand. Product changes that alter the performance of the product may occur of course, but those changes remain outside the boundaries of our analysis.

The Reprocessing Industry

The used products returned by consumers are transformed (by repair, scrapping, recycling, and so on) into usable secondhand products, parts, and raw materials or simply less harmful wastes. This transformation process may be performed by the original producers as a separate activity or by special firms. In the former case we distinguish between producers who already have a refund system and those who do not.

Producers with a refund system. In cases in which a producer-initiated profit-maximizing refund system already exists, though at a suboptimal level from society's point of view, we have firm profits as

$$\Pi = (\bar{b} - aX + eR_F - e'R)X - C_F X + g(R_F + R)X(V_F - R_F) \qquad (3\text{-}2)$$

where R_F is the producer refund and V_F is the producer's as well as the social valuation of a product return with $V_F = V \gtrless 0$. As in the market-generated case in the preceding chapter, we assume that there is no competition for the use of the returned products; thus the consumer gets only the refund from the producer regardless of the value of V. In contrast, the total optimal payment is given by $R + R_F = A + V$, where R $(=D)$ is the optimal government refund. The addition of a government deposit D equal to an extra refund R—with the deposit surplus still appearing as government revenue—has now only negative effects on demand. The reason is that all positive effects mentioned earlier and measured by $\bar{e}$ in equation (3-1) have already occurred in connection with the introduction of the producer refund, or the return disposal offer, and are included in $\bar{b}$. But the part of the output that is returned will increase by gR, thus giving a total return rate of $g(R_F + R)$. Now the firm will benefit from this effect, taken by itself if $V_F > R_F$; here V_F is assumed to be a reuse value only, not a net addition to profits from price differentiation. But it cannot compensate for the negative effect on demand, as we started out from an assumed profit maximum. When $V_F < R_F$, the firm would be subjected to a loss in addition to the one caused by the reduction in demand, provided of course that the firm is not compensated by the government.

In any case the introduction of the government deposit–refund system may influence the firm's own refund system. Because the government wants to have $R_F + R = A + V$, a change in R_F would have to be countered by a change in R, leaving the sum unaltered. Still, it may pay the firm to adjust R_F, as a change in R_F, $dR_F = - dR$, would affect profits by

$$dR_F(e + e')X - g(R_F + R)X \, dR_F = dR_F[e + e' - g(A + V)]X$$

before output is adjusted (see equation (3-2) above). Thus, if the net effect on demand, $e + e'$, due to a reduced deposit of $-dR$, exceeds the loss, $-g(A + V)$, due to the higher producer refund, an increase in R_F would increase profits, and *vice versa*. (The consumer will notice the distinction between R_F and R only indirectly by their different effects on gross price, but not when the product is returned.)

Producers without a refund system. If a producer without a refund system of his own were forced to accept returns of used products within a deposit–refund system, his profits would stay the same or decrease, if we assume that he had not overlooked the possibility of introducing a profitable refund system before the government introduced its system. Thus maximum profits after $D = R$ is introduced, $\Pi(X_P, R)$, with output optimally adjusted from X_A to X_P, are at most equal to maximum profits without the deposit–refund system, $\Pi(X_A)$. *A fortiori,* profits at the previously optimal output level

$$\Pi(X_A, R) \leq \Pi(X_P, R) \leq \Pi(X_A)$$

which for

$$\Pi(X_A, R) = (b - aX_A + \bar{e} - e'R)X_A - C_F X_A + gRX_A V_F$$

and

$$\Pi(X_A) = (b - aX_A)X_A - C_F X_A$$

implies that

$$\bar{e} - e'R + gRV_F \leq 0$$

Thus equilibrium output *ex ante* exceeds or equals equilibrium output *ex post;* that is, $X_A \geq X_P$, as

$$X_A = \frac{b - C_F}{2a}$$

and

$$X_P = \frac{b - C_F + (\bar{e} - e'R + gRV_F)}{2a}$$

Moreover, prices will change from

$$p_A = \frac{b + C_F}{2}$$

to

$$p_P = \frac{b + C_F + (\bar{e} - e'R + gRV_F)}{2} - 2gRV_F$$

This suggests that $p_P \gtrless p_A$ for $V_F < 0$ and that $p_P \leq p_A$ for $V_F = 0$. V cannot be positive here, as that would have implied that a producer-initiated refund system would have been worthwhile (see chapter 2). But it also cannot appear to the firm as a negative value under a government-initiated deposit–refund system, as we soon explain. Hence the only socially efficient case in which the original producer also is the firm processing the returned products—and has not been doing so from the beginning—is when the net reuse value to the firm, V_F, is zero. This means two things: first, the producer need not be "forced" to accept returns, as that in itself will not reduce profits, and, second, product prices will not increase ($p_P \leq p_A$).

The basis for this argument is the following: We recall (see figure 3-2) that, in general, consumers return products in government-initiated systems for a refund R and a scrap price, here called $V_c \gtreqless 0$. Returned products may be processed by the original producer F or by others, here called specialized treatment plants T. With a maximum net price bid from the treatment plants equal to V_T, the original producer would take care of the product returns only if he were willing to pay more than V_T. If V_F indicates his maximum net price bid and if $V_F > V_T$, the original producer would be the actual processing unit established by the market. V_T is assumed to be observable as a potential market price per unit returned, and the producer has to pay consumers $V_c = V_T$. Thus the consumer gets $R + V_c = R + V_T$ and the producer gets a profit per unit returned equal to $V_F{}^\Pi = V_F - V_T$.

$V_F{}^\Pi$ now has to be substituted for V_F in the expressions in the preceding paragraph where the case of $V_c = V_T \neq 0$ was not explicitly observed. But as we indicated there, $V_F{}^\Pi > 0$ would have led to a producer-initiated refund system. Thus what remains as a possible case in which the original producer also becomes the reprocessor is when $V_F{}^\Pi = 0$. This may be interpreted as the case in which the reprocessing industry as a whole is so competitive—or the advantage in reprocessing one's own products so insignificant—that V_F tends to equal V_T. The outcome is that $V_c = V_T = V_F = V$, the social reuse value, and that $D = R = A$ as before.

Specialized treatment plants. The case in which specialized treatment plants take care of the returned products is now obvious. If $V_T > V_F$, then the original producer is out of the reprocessing picture. And if the reprocessing industry is competitive, we would tend to have $V_c = V_T = V$. If not, that is if the reprocessing industry is a monopoly because of decreasing costs (such as in figure 3-2), we would have the same situation as when the original producer had a monopoly position and would have benefited from a refund system of his own. The two cases differ only with respect to the overall effects on profits. A profit-maximizing specialized reprocessing firm or industry cannot lose from the introduction of a deposit–refund system, as it will have emerged because of it, whereas the original producer may lose because of the demand effect, though not, as we have seen, because of his possibly choosing to be a reprocessing firm as well.[7]

In line with our discussion here we regard in the following the reprocessing industry (whether it contains the original producer or not) as one that is neither negatively affected by the introduction of a government-initiated deposit–refund system nor forced to accept and transform returned products from consumers. The reason for this view of the industry is that, regardless of whether the social reuse value V is positive or negative, the consumers will foot the bill. When $V < 0$, hence $V_c < 0$, the consumers will have to pay this amount by accepting a reduction in the refund. The reprocessing industry will then see to it that returned products are transformed into reusable products, raw materials, or less harmful wastes, whichever is most profitable, but at a long-term profit of zero. Granted this, we return to the analytically simpler main case with V and V_c assumed to be zero.

Free-lance Collectors

Aside from a specialized reprocessing industry, other new groups of economic agents may appear as a result of a deposit–refund system. One such group consists of firms or individuals who act as "free-lance" intermediary collectors, acquiring used units from consumers or picking them up if "common" property and turning them over to the reprocessing firms for a refund. This group may also be taken to include new secondhand users of refundable products who obtain these products in the way just indicated or by buying them from consumers with a higher $C_R{}^i$ and hence a lower net refund $R - C_R{}^i$. The origin of this group of free-lance collectors may be found in a difference in labor costs (or time costs) due to lower opportunity costs or large-scale collection and transportation technology or in a difference in information.

The effects of the emergence of this group could be great. The overall return costs of the system would diminish when people or firms with a small $C_R{}^i$ were substituted for those with a higher $C_R{}^i$. The activity of the

[7] This condition is based on the assumption, of course, that the government does not regulate entry, production, and prices in the reprocessing industry so that the most efficient structure cannot develop. This, however, is not a separate assumption but one derived from our basic assumption of an efficiency goal for the economy as a whole and is thus derived from the same source as the assumed choice of deposit and refund rates.

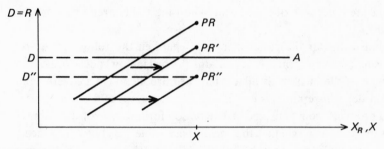

Figure 3-5.

free-lance collectors may also contribute to spreading the word that returns are possible and worthwhile; as a result, the return activity of consumers themselves may rise. In particular, this new group of collectors
may speed up the process of adjustment to the long-run return behavior
(see the PR_L curve in figure 3-2). Moreover, they may shorten the period
during which there are external effects from littering. Finally, their collection of other items not eligible for refunds but with a small scrap value
may turn out to be worthwhile because of low extra costs.

The effect on the optimal deposit–refund system may also be significant. The increased propensity to return used products to PR' in figure 3-5
will lead to a higher volume of returns with no effects on the optimal deposit rate when A is constant. But if the return level is already at 100 percent, or is brought to that, say, by a shift to PR'', the minimum optimal
deposit rate will be reduced to D'', disregarding the possible effect on X.

The free-lance collectors are a group of agents whose real income rises
as a consequence of the deposit–refund system. Thus there is no need to
pay particular attention to them in our subsequent analysis. They may be
included either as a part of the reprocessing industry or as a part of the
consumer group in line with the exposition in figure 3-5, that is, the consumers whose propensity to return used products is increased.

Pirate Producers of Refundable Products

A special group of agents may appear as a result of a deposit–refund system and have an adverse effect on the performance of the system. Especially when A, and hence D, is high, there may be an incentive to produce
"used" products or other refundable items solely for the purpose of collecting the refund. For example, bottles may be produced not for direct

use as beverage containers but for the purpose of being "sold" at a profit when "returned," or a primary underpriced metal may be turned directly into a scrap product with a high refund. This obviously presupposes that the deposit part of the deposit–refund system is badly designed or subject to low-cost abuses, as this "pirate" activity requires that deposit payments are absent or ineffective. As long as the reason is one of bad design, the problem is reduced to a need of sufficient foresight when the deposit–refund system is set up and to identifying the link in the production and distribution chain at which the deposit part is most easily administered without loopholes. But when a system design that precludes abuses turns out to entail high and perhaps prohibitive costs, the optimal version of the deposit–refund system may no longer be that suggested so far. "Unavoidable" risks of abuses may make it preferable to limit the deposit rate (say, below D or D'' in figure 3-5) if that eliminates or sufficiently reduces the pirate activity without also diminishing the return activity to an unacceptable level. Otherwise, only deposit–refund systems at the original deposit level remain as the best possible version.

What emerges from these observations is one possible drawback of the deposit–refund system, which has to be taken into account when the system is designed and when it is compared with alternative policy instruments.[8] In the latter context we may note, however, that there are alternatives such as subsidies ($=A$) that would encourage abuses of the kind now mentioned even more.

Effects on Government

Before analyzing the effects on consumers, we observe some of the options open to the policy administration and their implications for the government. So far in this chapter the deposit–refund system has been viewed as one in which the government levies a mandatory deposit on products with a disposal or reuse problem and, after having defined a certain transformation activity or a certain end product from reprocessing, transfers funds to be used as refunds to those firms that take on the reprocessing job. We have just indicated that the production or selling link where the deposit obligation is introduced would have to be chosen with respect to possible

[8] It should be added, though, that it is not easy to come up with examples of such large-scale abuses that would constitute a real threat to the efficiency of the system. It is difficult, for example, to imagine a fraudulent large-scale delivery of containers or batteries going on unobserved for a significant period of time.

risks for abuse as well as to administrative costs for government and the agents involved. In principle, there is no difference in operational technique and administrative analysis between a deposit–refund system and the combination of an excise tax (the deposit part) and a unit subsidy (the refund part) or a net excise tax when the original producer does the reprocessing.

In determining the optimal deposit rates, we have mentioned the role of the alternative cost of nonreturn of the product considered for a deposit–refund system and the policy costs of different system designs. In addition, we have to observe the particular consequences of a system in which the return is less than 100 percent and hence a surplus of deposits over refunds appears. For example, this surplus could be used as a substitute for other forms of government finance, which would be of great value for an economy with imperfect, distortive tax systems. Or it could be used for nondistortive compensatory payments to losers in the deposit–refund system, such as certain producers.[9]

Leaving the distribution aspects aside for the moment, we note another optional use of the surplus that is likely to emerge from deposit–refund systems as so far described. When the distance in time between deposit and refund payments for a given product unit is substantial and when the deposit–refund system refers to an already existing consumption activity, we have a time delay problem concerning the refund part and hence the benefit part of the system. For example, deposits introduced on cars, refrigerators, and similar durables would have no effect on disposal behavior for a very long period to come. A possible extension of a deposit–refund system in a situation like this would be to introduce at the same time a subsidy on returns of units already in use and hence affect disposal behavior up to the time when the deposit–refund system comes into a full effect. The result is of course a windfall income to those who own products already in use (if the subsidy is not combined with some temporary tax to avoid this particular consequence). But given that the policy costs of the refund part of the deposit–refund system are already there (though the present value of these costs may now be significantly increased), such an addition to the deposit–refund system may prove to be the most efficient policy measure with respect to the near-future disposal or reuse problem. Moreover, from a financial point of view, the deposit–refund

[9] Or it could be used for reducing the deposit rates to a level below that of the refund rates. But, as can be readily seen, that would remove certain characteristics of the deposit–refund system that have been crucial for the analysis here and would make us deal with what is essentially an ordinary subsidy system.

system may turn out to be the only politically feasible way to fund a program that aims at a resolution of the short-term reuse-disposal problem.

Although the deposit–refund system and the temporary subsidy of returns of predeposit units are two separate issues, the policy cost and government revenue aspects make it relevant to consider the combination of the two as a special version of a deposit–refund system. Now, if the stock of the refundable products has been increasing over time and will continue to do so after a possible temporary setback as a result of the introduction of deposits, the total inflow of deposits will be large enough to cover the outflow of refunds (subsidies) in each period, given that the optimal real refunds do not change substantially over time (for example, because of product changes and hence changes in optimal deposits over time). However, we must now take into account the interest aspect on deposits, given the long-term nature of the deposit–refund system under consideration. In the simplest case with one and the same interest rate r relevant for all agents in the economy including the government, the preceding analysis simply requires that the refund at time $T + t$ for a unit bought at time T is

$$R(T + t) = D(T)(1 + r)^t \qquad (3\text{-}3)$$

If so, and with $R(T + t) = A(T + t)$ constant over time, deposits paid at time T, $D(T)$, will be below refunds paid at time T, $R(T)$, for units bought prior to time T. Thus, for example, if the volume of new products sold were equal to the volume of used products returned at time T, the inflow of deposits would not cover the outflow of refunds (subsidies). Only if

$$X_R(T)R(T) \leq X(T)D(T) = X(T)\frac{R(T + t)}{(1 + r)^t} \qquad T = 0, 1, 2, \ldots \qquad (3\text{-}4)$$

that is,

$$X_R(T)(1 + r)^t \leq X(T) \quad \text{for} \quad R(T) = R(T + t)$$

would the total deposit–refund budget not be underbalanced in any period. This requires, for example, that $X(T)$ grows by at least $100r$ percent per period, if all used products are returned, or that the fraction of units returned is at most $1/(1 + r)^t$, if $X(T)$ is constant over time.

The special version of the deposit–refund system now discussed will run into financial problems if the product quality is changed over time such that the reuse or disposal value of the product, sold at time T, $A(T$

$+ t)$, drops to zero. In this case, or in the case in which production of the commodity is discontinued, there will eventually be no deposits (at least no efficient deposits) to finance the refunds on the outstanding stock of products for which the reuse or disposal value is still positive. Here the subsidy that was added to and financed by the original deposit–refund system will create a financial problem at a later stage. Moreover, an optimal version of the enlarged deposit–refund system might require additional funding at an earlier stage, that is, when condition (3-4) is not fulfilled. Then, if the deposit budget is taken to be a binding constraint on the enlarged system, a second-best version of the whole enlarged deposit–refund system will have to be defined. This may be one in which refunds (subsidies) during earlier or all periods are set below $A(t)$ or deposits are raised above the level given by equation (3-3), or both.

Although we do not investigate the details of this second-best version here, we note that the high shadow price of government funds in these cases may be expressed as a low real interest rate for government funds (r_g). A lower r_g would reflect an increased preference for having government funds available now instead of later. Moreover, a lower r_g inserted into equation (3-3) would bring about the rise in deposits just mentioned, to a level above $D(T) = R(T + t)/(1 + r_c)^t$, where r_c is the interest rate relevant for the consumer. This divergence of interest rates and, in particular, $r_c > r_g$ may arise under other circumstances as well. One case is when credit markets are imperfect, so that certain consumers cannot borrow or so that consumer borrowing rates and perhaps even consumer lending rates are substantially higher than relevant government interest rates. Another case is when it is difficult (or prohibitively expensive) to establish when a certain item was bought and hence when the deposit actually was paid. This may be the case with inexpensive products bought in large quantities over time and kept for long periods, perhaps because of fixed return costs (see chapter 2). Here the refund should be set close to or equal to the deposit rate, which might require an interest rate (r_g) for the individual deposit–refund period far below the relevant consumer rate of interest. For reasons such as these, we must observe, in particular, the consequences of $r_c > r_g$ as we look at the overall effects of the deposit–refund system from the point of view of the consumers.

Consumers

The remaining group of agents to discuss is the consumers of the products on which deposits are introduced. As was indicated in the demand section, they may all lose or all gain, or some may gain and others lose from the deposit–refund system. We may note in passing that the subgroup of consumers that we called free-lance collectors, including certain second-hand users of the products, would all gain. But for the group as a whole, everyone would be certain to gain only if $C_d{}^i > C_R{}^i$, with the same cost difference for all. The saving in disposal costs would of course tend to increase demand and hence market prices, but not enough that the price increase would outweigh the gain of $C_d{}^i - C_R{}^i$ per unit. In this case the optimal deposit is zero, and there is a 100 percent return rate. Moreover, producers as producers of the product would also gain in this case, barring large increases in administrative costs for bookkeeping, transfer, and control of deposits.

If, instead, $C_d{}^i < C_R{}^i$, the cost difference again being the same for everyone, all consumers would lose, being only partly compensated by the ensuing price decrease. As we saw in figure 3-4, deposits would now be D^*, just above $C_R - C_d{}^i$, and all consumers would choose the return alternative.[10] Here also producers would lose from the introduction of a deposit–refund system.

In cases in which disposal cost differences are heterogeneous, or sufficiently so, some consumers lose and others gain. For the purpose of illustration, let us take the case in which there are two consumer groups 1 and 2, cost differences are the same within each group, and $C_d{}^1 > C_R{}^1$ and $C_d{}^2 < C_R{}^2$. If cost differences for groups 1 and 2 are as in the two preceding homogeneous cases, respectively, group 1 must win and win by more than it did in the first homogeneous case. The reason is of course that prices now will not increase as much, if at all. The fact that we may now have an optimal $D = D^* > 0$ does not have any effect on these consumers (interest aspects aside). Group 2 will always lose—by more than in the second homogeneous case for $D = D^*$, as prices will not drop as much, if at all. It will also lose if optimal $D = 0$ (a pure return system) because of the price increase that then would occur. Return rates will be 100 percent except in the latter case, where this is true only for group 1. Because the price change (Δp) may be positive or negative, producers may gain or lose from the deposit–refund system in a heterogeneous case.

Increasing the heterogeneity of disposal cost differences will not affect the nature of these conclusions except that, in general, optimal D now will be strictly positive and the return rate will be less than 100 percent. Here

[10] This is provided that D^* (for example, the externality avoided) exceeds A. Otherwise, a deposit–refund system would not be introduced.

the individual consumer will lose at most $D + \Delta p$, in terms of net price per unit. Hence the maximum losers will be those consumers who have $C_R{}^i - C_d{}^i > R$ in a situation in which the weighted average $C_R{}^i - C_d{}^i < 0$ for all consumers is very small, giving rise to a substantial price increase. In other words, we are likely to have some individual losers with significant losses in a deposit–refund system with a large A, where the range of $C_R{}^i - C_d{}^i$ is wide and the distribution skewed toward low (negative) disposal cost differences.

These results remain unchanged when we deal explicitly with long-term deposit–refund systems in which $R(t) = D(0) (1 + r)^t$ and interest rates are identical for all agents involved. Given substantial interest rate differences between consumer rates $r_c{}^i$ and r_g and given that $R(t) = D(0)$ $(1 + r_g)^t$, where $r_g = 0$ is a possible special case, additional effects on consumers (actually on consumers as creditors in the deposit–refund system) will appear. When $r_c{}^i > r_g$, the consumer will find the deposit rate to be too great for the given refund prospect in relation to alternative uses of credit open to him. Thus the consumer will lose (also) as creditor. This may occur in particular if there are high costs for identifying when deposits were paid, if there are imperfect credit markets with credit restrictions, or if r_g is low for other reasons of "imperfection" in the economy. In the probably less interesting case in which $r_c{}^i < r_g$, the credit part will help to compensate for the losses the individual makes in the pure consumer role or add to his gains. As we have designed the government deposit–refund system, producers are not affected by the credit and interest aspects of the problem.

Conclusion

We now sum up the effects on all groups of agents in the economy, that is, on all the different economic roles of the individuals influenced by the deposit–refund system: the buyers of the product on which a deposit is introduced, the target group of beneficiaries of the policy program, the owners of firms producing or reprocessing the product, the taxpayers, and the creditors.

To begin with, we identify an obvious group of winners, the agents defined as the *beneficiaries* of a reduction in external effects, an increased future supply of primary products, or other factors that explain why certain ways of product disposal are penalized by the deposit–refund system. Owners of specialized *treatment firms* are also winners. *Taxpayers,* too, are winners whenever the deposit–refund system provides a surplus and hence a substitute for tax revenue.

A second group of agents consists of the *consumers* of the product and the *owners of the firms* producing the product. In this group, all may gain or all may lose, or, in the general case, some may gain and others lose. The main losers are to be found among consumers whose costs for returning the product exceed the costs for the disposal alternative otherwise used. They may prefer either to forgo the refund (if $R < C_R{}^i - C_d{}^i$) or to accept the more expensive disposal alternative (if $R > C_R{}^i - C_d{}^i$), the latter being more likely the higher is $A = D$. Their losses would be still higher if there were enough consumers who gained from the deposit–refund system, $C_R{}^i < C_d{}^i$, and made aggregate demand go up, thereby increasing prices. Under other circumstances the owners of the producing firms might be substantial losers.

For all losers, high individual or average $C_R{}^i$ plays a crucial role. As the government may want to compensate the losers, a possibly efficient redistribution device would be to subsidize collection costs C_R or to provide collection services, in particular to those consumer groups with large $C_R{}^i - C_d{}^i$ differences, when it is feasible to distinguish such groups (such as by region). As a result, there would be a reduced likelihood that demand and hence product prices would go down; if so, firm owners would tend to be unharmed by the introduction of the deposit–refund system. Otherwise, firms could be compensated fairly easily by direct lump-sum payments, a redistribution solution less likely to be practicable for losing consumers. If sufficient transfer payments of the two kinds mentioned could be made from the deposit surplus (which would reduce the taxpayer's gain) or by increased general taxes when the beneficiaries of the policy proper are people in general or easily discernible taxpayer groups, the transfer would be made without creating a new group of losers.

If deposits were made for long periods and if refunds were set at a level below that which is required with respect to consumer interest rates, consumers would lose in their role of *creditors*. However, if this kind of redistribution is not acceptable to the government, refunds will not be set in this way. In other words, consumers as creditors do not lose unless the government intentionally makes such a redistribution of real income.

To sum up, the major concern from a distribution point of view centers on certain consumers of the product and on owners of producing firms. In the real world, however, agents or roles as defined here are combined to varying degrees in one and the same person. In each concrete application of a deposit–refund system, the extent to which individuals lose as consumers or owners of producer firms and gain in other capacities must be determined before specific compensatory actions are taken. For example, it may be that individuals who tend to lose as buyers of the product get a compensation as taxpayers or as beneficiaries of the policy program (even when the beneficiaries appear only at a future date).

DEPOSIT–REFUND SYSTEMS AND ALTERNATIVE POLICY SOLUTIONS

As was pointed out in our discussion of consumer-paid deposit–refund systems in the preceding section, a straightforward efficiency-directed system might not benefit all individuals in the economy. But we also learned that there are certain options for redistributive measures, although they need not be regarded as sufficient by the government. This is of course a pattern we observe in almost all discussions of policy measures aimed at reaching specific efficiency objectives. The question now is whether there are alternative policy instruments for the particular problems and objectives given that outdo the deposit–refund system and, if so, under what general conditions this would be true.

Subsidies

Subsidizing returns to reprocessing units directly—or indirectly by, for example, subsidizing the output of such units and allowing them to offer a sufficient scrap price—could bring about the same disposal pattern as under a deposit–refund system. The main advantage is the lack of administrative costs for the deposit part of the deposit–refund system. But a possible drawback exists from the efficiency point of view; pirate (but now formally legal) producers for the disposal market would be more difficult to exclude once the possibility of deposits, or other "taxes" assumed to be levied on all producers, is ruled out. This situation might call for stricter constraints on subsidies to avoid abuses than would be needed for the refunds in a deposit–refund·system.

The main difference, however, would probably be in distribution. There would be no possible losers now among the producers of the product. But consumers would lose for whom $C_R{}^i > C_d{}^i$ and for whom the ensuing price increase (due to increased demand from subsidized disposal costs) would outweigh the net value of the subsidy. In fact, this group would tend to be larger, as the price increase would be higher now than under a deposit–refund system, given a subsidy such that payments for returns would equal $A + V$. Moreover, a new group of losers would emerge, the taxpayers. Thus, in comparison with the deposit–refund system (without corrective redistribution measures), taxpayers and certain buyers of the product would lose to the owners of the producing firms. Aside from possible political constraints that might make it difficult for the government to consider the subsidy alternative in the first place, these distributional effects may appear less attractive to the government than those of the deposit–refund system.

Taxes or Charges

Another theoretically possible alternative to a deposit–refund system is to introduce charges on nonreturns. As we have already pointed out, the practicality of this approach is limited by the difficulties in observing the behavior of not returning used products. In most cases of nonreturns, such as littering, dumping, and voluntary leakages, costs of detection are prohibitively high. The alternative approach of keeping records of items bought and not returned within a certain period of time, searching, and billing the consumers would hardly be much less expensive. Thus, on the grounds of comparative policy costs, a system of charges cannot be found to be superior to a consumer-paid deposit–refund system except for possible special cases.

Regulation

The remaining alternative—and perhaps the obvious alternative—to be discussed here is regulation or prohibition of "improper" disposal. If such a rule included fines on detected and prosecuted cases of violation, we would in fact have a system of stochastic charges (aside from the nonmonetary aspects of the penalties). The expected value of such charges on firms may, at least in principle, be set at such a high level that the result would be the same as in the case of charges on all nonreturns. However, because the individual consumer can be expected to be able to influence the risks of being detected, time and other resources would be spent on an activity that is socially nonproductive. Moreover, the fines required under such circumstances would often be quite high, so high that they may be ruled out on grounds of justice, given that people could break the rules by "mistake," lack of information, and so on. Thus a regulatory system relying mainly on fining detected violators would have its limitations.

If, on the other hand, the regulatory system is not enforced by fines or other forms of punishment, the field is wide open for speculation about the merits of this system in relation to those of the deposit–refund system. All that can be said then is that the deposit–refund system provides economic incentives to reach a given policy goal, whereas this kind of regulation does not.

Product Charges?

Our discussion of policy alternatives has excluded product charges, an instrument often proposed in these areas. The reason is found in our requirement that we should deal only with instruments that reduce "improper" disposal to an extent similar to that accomplished in a deposit–refund system. A product charge, that is, a tax on all products in the amount of average social costs not covered by price (such as average waste management costs and external costs of littering), would reduce improper disposal only via its effect of reducing demand for the product, as it does not differentiate between disposal alternatives. In addition, however, product charges would be sure to worsen the position of both consumers and producers by raising product prices for consumers and lowering net producer prices (given some elasticity of demand and costs). At the same time, it would raise government revenue in the same way as the deposit–refund system, that is, to cover actual external costs, and so on, provided average social costs equal marginal social costs.

SUMMARY

In this chapter we have dealt with consumer-paid deposits on products whose traditional disposal involves negative external effects or waste of underpriced resources (underpriced because of political constraints). The reuse or scrap value of the waste product that a market has or would have established will be suboptimal under these circumstances. And if a market-generated deposit–refund system existed, it would be suboptimal for the same reasons. Thus government intervention may be required. This policy issue has been discussed here on the assumption that, in general, the social reuse or scrap value V equals zero.

With a refund equal to the externality avoided or equal to the difference between the shadow price and the market price of a resource (for example, a secondary metal) or a refund determined by long-run economies of scale in the reprocessing industry and slow adjustment in disposal behavior or simply by merit want valuations by government, a socially efficient change in disposal behavior and reuse may be accomplished. The introduction of a government-initiated deposit–refund system—in which deposits equal to the (present value of) refunds are directly or indirectly channeled through government—could, as we have seen, increase or decrease demand, price, and output of the original good. In such deposit–refund systems—in contrast to the market-generated ones and government-initiated extensions thereof—consumers receive a refund as well as a "scrap" price (V_c) $\gtrless 0$ for the products returned. V_c tends to equal V provided there is perfect competition in the reprocessing industry. And this industry may or may not include the producer(s) of the original product. Thus, in government-initiated systems, the original producer may be required to accept product returns but can avoid being the actual reprocessor of the returned products if this would cause losses to him.

Aside from the reprocessing firms, another new group of agents may appear that increases the efficiency of the system. These are the free-lance collectors, who have low net collection costs and who may speed up the adjustment process. Pirate producers may also appear, who reduce the efficiency of the system by producing "disposal" products in order to collect the refunds and avoid paying the deposits. Such incentives would exist if the refund (and V_c) exceeded the production cost and if the government deposit requirements were ineffective. But the chances for such pirates to operate unnoticed on a large scale are hardly significant enough to jeopardize the efficiency of the deposit–refund system.

We may summarize the main effects on distribution by reference to a set of diagrams intended for the more technically interested reader (figures 3-6 and 3-7). Given that a competitive reprocessing industry establishes a $V_c = V$, the effects of a deposit–refund system with the same difference $C_R{}^i - C_d{}^i = \Delta C > 0$ for all consumers are visualized in figure 3-6. With marginal social costs of nonreturn A assumed to be constant and larger than ΔC, the refund should be set equal to ΔC, or just above, to ensure that all units will be returned. As all deposits are canceled out by refunds, demand is reduced by ΔC, assuming that the increase in disposal costs ΔC shows up as a decrease in demand prices for the product. Moreover, if we assume that demand equals compensated demand, the area a in figure 3-6 will show the loss of aggregate consumer surplus at the initial

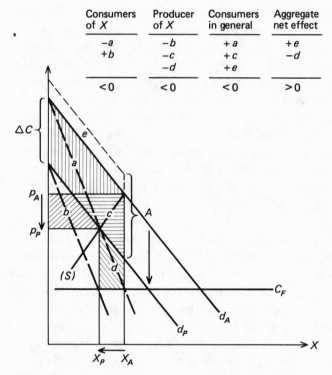

Consumers of X	Producer of X	Consumers in general	Aggregate net effect
$-a$	$-b$	$+a$	$+e$
$+b$	$-c$	$+c$	$-d$
	$-d$	$+e$	
<0	<0	<0	>0

Figure 3-6.

price p_A. The demand shift reduces price to p_P, which makes consumers gain area b from a *monopoly* producer, who in addition loses c and d. Because all products are returned, marginal social costs in the amount of A are eliminated. If we add A to the new demand curve (d_P), the total value of social costs avoided, and thus the gains by consumers in general, is areas $a + c + e$. The net aggregate gain can be seen to be $e - d$. Thus A must be sufficiently much larger than ΔC for the net gain to be positive, provided that we want to include the reduction in monopoly profits as we have done here.

If the monopoly is replaced by a *competitive industry* with a supply curve S, d disappears, and producer losses now marked by c are reduced to the area above S, leaving a net aggregate gain of e plus the area of c below S.

The illustration of our main case, in which $C_R{}^i - C_d{}^i$ differs among consumers as shown by the PR curves in figure 3-7, is less comprehensive.

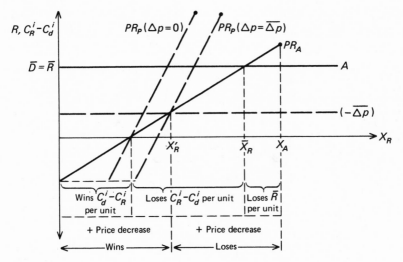

Figure 3-7.

But given that the individual consumer has no influence on the price of the product, optimal $\bar{D} = \bar{R}$ must equal A. The effect on prices now depends on the size relation between demand from consumers with $C_R^i - C_d^i < 0$ whose demand increases and demand from consumers with $C_R^i - C_d^i > 0$ whose demand is reduced. The initial effect on demand is reflected by the shift from PR_A to PR_P ($\Delta p = 0$). With, say, a net decrease in aggregate demand and hence a price reduction of $\Delta \bar{p}$, consumers of units up to X'_R in figure 3-7 experience a decline, and those above X'_R experience an increase in net prices. Producers lose when demand decreases (and *vice versa*), and taxpayers win, as all deposits are not refunded.[11]

We have also seen that for deposit–refund systems extending over long periods and for a government rate of discount lower than the relevant consumer rate of discount, consumers will lose in their role of creditors, that is, in lending the deposits to government until the date of the refund. But the result that certain individuals may lose in their role of creditors, consumers, or owners of firms producing the deposit–refund-regulated product must be balanced against positive distributional effects on the same individuals, as beneficiaries of the policy program, as taxpayers, and as owners of reprocessing firms in the short run.

[11] The reader should be reminded of the assumption made here that $C_R^i - C_d^i$ is perceived by everyone as a price change.

4 PRODUCER-PAID SYSTEMS AND SUBSTITUTES

INTRODUCTION

As we indicated in the introduction to the preceding chapter, there are cases in which producers pay deposits to other producers and are given refunds upon the return of the product or a certain part of it. Producer-paid systems, like consumer-paid systems, may be market-generated or government-initiated. The market-generated refund systems for purchases by producers may involve the same products as consumers buy, such as beverage containers used in restaurants, or they may involve specific producer goods, such as containers for railway freight. The government-initiated systems may be introduced for the reasons we discussed in the preceding chapter, that is, external effects or waste management costs of present disposal patterns imposed on the general public, second-best pricing formulas for primary products, incentive reinforcing mechanisms, and the existence of merit wants.

In general, the same kind of analysis is applicable to producers in these cases as was used for consumers in the market-generated and government-initiated systems discussed in chapters 2 and 3. There may be substantial and systematic differences in certain variables, however, such as in the sign or size of $C_R - C_d$, that will have important practical consequences. Moreover, there may be systematic differences in policy costs that may affect the relative merits of deposit–refund systems and of their "competitors" from a policy point of view. For example, it may be easier to detect "littering" by a few large producers than by many small consumers, and this may improve the relative position of policy solutions such as regulations or charges levied on detrimental behavior (see the discussion of policy alternatives in chapter 3).[1]

The case of large producers operating on the buyer's side of deposit–refund systems is likely to have other particular consequences as well. This is obvious first of all when firms are large enough to play a monopolistic or monopsonistic role within the deposit–refund system. But, in addition, the size of the producer may affect the deposit–refund system in a more direct way. It may no longer be efficient for the deposits to be paid in cash by large firms; instead, banks may appear as financial intermediaries in one way or another. In fact, it may be beneficial to modify the deposit–refund system even further and let an insurance system replace the version of the deposit–refund system discussed so far. In a later section of this chapter we deal with these credit and insurance aspects.

So far, we have pointed out some features of producer-paid systems that may differ from consumer-paid systems, though in degree more than in kind. We now turn to government-initiated systems that are applicable only to producers and that present more specific analytical problems. We also turn from practical applications primarily in the fields of environmental protection and conservation policy to practical applications primarily in the field of consumer policy.

The government may wish to intervene in the self-generated distribution of rights and liabilities between producers and consumers. This intervention may consist in part of introducing deposit–refund systems or variants thereof, such as product guarantees and producer liability to accept used products for disposal (and give a refund, as the case may be), cases we have discussed to some extent above. But in addition, producers may be required to guarantee the permanency of their liability in these respects or to provide a compensatory substitute, even after they are out of business, to the extent that such liability remains (for uncompleted contracts, durable goods, and so on). The emphasis of this chapter will be

---

[1] It should be noted, however, that in several cases even large companies have tried illegally to dump large quantities of toxic or hazardous products. For example, in 1977 a large chemical firm in Sweden was found to have been burying barrels of highly toxic material that then began to leak out into waterways. A more well-known case is the oil spillage from the cleaning of tankers at sea.

on the form and effects of such liability arrangements when backed up by
a producer-paid deposit–refund system or some variant thereof.

In the first sections of this chapter we discuss in more detail the use of
deposit–refund systems for producer liability arrangements. Then we observe the problem of choosing between deposits in cash and insurance. In
the final section we extend the analysis to include the particular services
produced by government and discuss the role of deposit–refund systems
and similar liability arrangements for such services.

PRODUCER LIABILITY
AND DEPOSIT–REFUND SYSTEMS

Even in a market economy with a minimum of government intervention
there may be a tendency to supply commodities with some degree of producer liability for products sold to consumers.[2] Informal procedures may
have developed so that deficient commodities are replaced when certain
faults appear in the product. Or firms may offer formal guarantees of
product performance with more or less strict limitations on the length
and scope of the guarantees. The reason for such market-generated transfers of liability from consumers to profit-maximizing producers is of
course that producers have found that such measures stimulate demand
or reduce the risk of government intervention. In other words, informal replacements of faulty products and compensation payments may pay off in
the sense that cost increases today are outweighed by future increases in
revenue. And formal guarantees may prove to be an effective marketing
device for which future cost increases are outweighed by increased revenue today.

Market-generated producer liability may affect consumer choice in
several ways. First, it may turn out that different producers sell physically
identical products with an optional guarantee for an increase in price or
even with different sets of guarantees at different prices. Given perfect information on the consumer side and given different consumer preferences

[2] For a general discussion of producer liability and its economic effects, see
Roland N. McKean, "Product Liability: Implications of Some Changing Property
Rights," *Quarterly Journal of Economics* vol. 84 (November/December 1970) pp.
611–626. See also Nina W. Cornell, Roger G. Noll, and Barry Weingast, *Safety
Regulation,* in Henry Owen and Charles L. Schultze, *Setting National Priorities*
(Washington, D.C., Brookings Institution, 1976) pp. 463–477.

with respect to guarantees, the result will be increased consumer choice and increased consumer welfare when the price of the basic nonguaranteed product is not raised. However, with a higher price for the basic product or with imperfect consumer information, there is no clear conclusion as to the effects on consumer welfare. Second, it may turn out that the basic product disappears from the market, leaving only products with, say, a uniformly designed guarantee. If the reason for this result is that all consumers had perfect information and all preferred the more expensive guaranteed product to the cheaper basic product, the result is again one of unambiguously improved consumer welfare. But with imperfect information and especially with different consumer preferences, the outcome is unclear. In fact, if some consumers with perfect information actually prefer the cheaper basic product, but that product is taken off the market because of economies of scale, these consumers at least would lose from the introduction of producer liability.

Government-initiated guarantee requirements, either by consumer protection laws against faulty products in general or by specific regulations on particular products, have similar effects. It is often emphasized by business that the resulting price increases accompanying the extended producer liability from government intervention may lead to negative net effects for consumers. It follows from what we said above that the actual outcome of nonoptional guarantees depends on consumer preferences and consumer information. In some cases of government-initiated compulsory guarantees, some consumers lose, such as well-informed consumers who prefer the cheaper basic product. Only if the government has optional guarantees introduced without any effect on the price of the basic product would consumers be sure not to lose (possible future effects on product design being disregarded).

So far we have taken for granted that guaranteed products will be more expensive than those without a guarantee. Given that product quality remains the same, that there are no economies of scale, and that there are product returns under the guarantee system, this is true simply for the reason of an induced increase in demand. But as we saw in chapter 2 (pages 12–14, we may expect in addition that the producer will try to make the product more costly in order to reduce product returns under the guarantee system. For certain kinds of guarantees, however, we may expect product quality and unit costs to remain unchanged. For example, guarantees giving consumers the unlimited right to return certain durable products within a week or so after purchase (during a "cooling-off" period) will probably not induce changes in product quality. And guarantees of spare part availability[3] will hardly affect product design; if anything, they may provide incentives to make products or product parts less durable and less expensive. But in other cases, it is reasonable to expect that changes in product quality will occur. These changes may be small, such as when producers find it worthwhile to reduce product failure by testing the product before it is marketed. Or they may be quite extensive, such as when firms redesign products to improve durability. And in some cases, guarantee systems may provide such strong incentives for product quality changes that the original product is replaced by an altogether new one, making *ex ante* and *ex post* prices noncomparable. Thus it is neither correct nor meaningful to argue that prices always will rise as a consequence of a guarantee imposed by government. Although we continue to assume that guarantees of product performance are coupled with price increases, we know now that there are exceptions to this rule.

A kind of guarantee not mentioned so far in this section is the case of producer liability for the disposal of the product. If not part of a deposit–refund system with strictly positive deposits and refunds, this becomes the return-but-no-refund case mentioned in chapter 2. A government-initiated disposal guarantee of this kind for a given product that lacks a positive reuse value would tend to increase prices as producer costs and perhaps also demand increase.

An issue closely related to the disposal issue is the restoration of production sites after production is discontinued. Performance bonds on firms that otherwise may leave abandoned sites with accident risks for children and eyesores for neighbors and others are often used to reduce these problems. Production units in urban as well as in rural areas may be involved, strip-mining and junk yards being particularly important examples. Whenever the bond requires the firm to restore the site in a given fashion, the firm's restoration costs can be expected to influence the investment design as well as the way production is carried out, both of which would promote overall efficiency.[4] This kind of guarantee—a guarantee

---

[3] Attempts to establish such guarantees exist in the European Community, for example. See the Commission of the European Communities (CED), *Consumer Protection and Information Policy* (Brussels, 1977) p. 67.

[4] Let us note in passing that when the producer does not have the final responsibility, such as when the firm simply has to pay a fee per unit of output during the operation period for restoration work to be conducted by the government, restoration costs will not be internalized and allowed to influence the production design.

of a maximum limit to detrimental external effects—can also be expected to raise product prices.

Now, the above-mentioned guarantee systems, especially if initiated by the government, would cause concern if producer (seller) liability and hence consumer protection vanished should the producer (seller) go bankrupt. This problem is absent in the case of performance bonds, where the validity of guarantees is secured by a deposit or by a commitment arranged with a bank. The risk that a contract might not be fulfilled would of course be particularly important if the guarantee system created conditions favorable for hit-and-run firms, that is, firms making profits out of commitments they never intend to meet because they plan to put themselves out of business.[5] But even when firms in fact try to stay in business and try to fulfill their obligations, bankruptcies and consumer damages may occur. If it is a government policy goal to protect consumers under such contingencies (say, the government finds it unreasonable that consumers should be required to make probability estimates of bankruptcy risks), there are two alternative routes to take. The government could either take over the responsibility in case of bankruptcy (which is now often the case on a pure *ad hoc* basis in more spectacular instances of consumer damage) or make the producer or seller provide collateral for existing commitments beyond bankruptcy.

The latter case is a new instance of deposit–refund systems. Here producers might be forced to pay deposits covering guarantees offered or other commitments made either voluntarily or in abiding by laws and regulations. The system could operate essentially like a tax system; that is, it could be based on liability statements supplied by firms, with government control being exercised on a sample basis with a higher probability of control for certain producer groups, such as those with whom a higher hit-and-run tendency may exist. For the system to work properly, the

[5] To take a concrete case, there has been since 1974 a law in the United Kingdom regulating proper building, conversion, or enlargement of buildings that makes builders responsible for a period of six years after completion of the work (see CED, *Consumer Protection,* p. 31). Obviously, this kind of legislation could be quite ineffective if there were a large number of (small) contractors staying in the market for only short periods of time. As another example, the Swedish Consumer Protection Agency (Konsumentverket) has pointed out in a review of the proposals made by a government commission on bankruptcy laws that it is important to note that consumers make losses from bankruptcies, for example, by forfeiting their down payments on products bought. It appears, the agency says, that in some cases bankruptcy is used intentionally as a profit-making instrument (see the journal published by the agency, *Konsumenträtt & Ekonomi,* no 3 (1979) p. 48).

amount of deposits would have to be adjusted to changes in the producer's debt position *vis à vis* consumers. If the producer goes out of business, the consumer (or the government, as the case may be) is protected by compensatory payments from this fund of deposits.

A deposit–refund system of this kind could be useful whenever each separate part of the commitments made by or forced upon a producer cannot be paid on a *quid pro quo* basis, as in the case of construction contracts with installment payments after delivery or after fulfillment of each part of the contract. In other words, it is potentially useful provided that transaction costs or the insurance features of the guarantee make it necessary for the buyer to make payments in advance of the final realization of all commitments made to him by the seller. However, a consequence of the government's requirement that firms pay deposits to be refunded after the commitments are fulfilled, or arrangements to the same effect, may be that the producer changes the payment structure or even the product, that is, the package of services offered. Such changes could be found to be profitable even to the extent that all advance payments have been eliminated, making an actual application of the deposit–refund system superfluous in those instances.

In many countries, government has introduced requirements for product safety and imposed constraints on the environmental impact of new commodities. Whenever the fulfillment of such conditions has to be checked by a government agency before the product is marketed, tests of the product will have to be made or controlled by the agency. Especially when the product may have long-term effects or may perform in new ways after a long period of use, these tests or controls may take considerable time. Cycles in application inflow and inflexible adjustment of the testing or screening capacity of the agency may add to the delay.[6] In other coun-

---

[6] These problems can be observed, for example, on the Swedish market for medical drugs. The government agency (Socialstyrelsen) responsible for checking new medicines before they are released on the market has been unable to keep review time short. In 1979, for example, 800 reports on side effects of new drugs were waiting to be handled; this is said to imply a six-month delay in dealing with reports coming in. In some cases, important new drugs are delayed a year or more for reasons of "unnecessary bureaucracy." The main reason is said to be lack of personnel (or lack of means to offer salaries for competent people). A government proposal has been advanced according to which new drugs could be released earlier under certain provisions, such as that prescriptions can be made only by specialists or used only in certain specialized clinics (see the Stockholm newspaper, *Dagens Nyheter*, February 22, 1979). The fact that a government could advocate an earlier release with certain additional safeguards is important for the application of deposit–refund systems to be discussed here.

tries or other instances, the government has preferred not to impose strict regulations before the product is marketed, leaving the "proof of the pudding to be found in the eating" and taking action only if and when sufficient evidence has accumulated more or less automatically.

Both of these alternative procedures have drawbacks, especially if the company itself has tested the product and thus is in possession of valuable product information, although the quality of the information may be questioned by nonpartisan groups. In the first case of strict government regulation *ex ante,* the producer may "know" that the product meets the requirements but has to wait for others to reconfirm his findings. In the case of *ex post* regulation, the producer may "know" or suspect on grounds of his particular expertise in the field that the product will not meet certain requirements that probably will be introduced and enforced in the long run. But in this case the producer may still find it profitable to market the product and sell it as long as possible.

In both these cases the option exists for the government to transfer certain liability to producers of new commodities and enforce this liability by a financial responsibility.[7] Thus the firm may be allowed to market the product by making a deposit (or by fulfilling a similar obligation; see below) determined by court or the government agency involved. This can be regarded as alternative to *ex ante* regulation, because failure to comply with the rules concerning the deposit makes it illegal to market the product. But the fact that a producer is given the right to sell new products without first having the government sanction the products resembles the case of *ex post* regulation.

Uncertainty may in some cases be so great that the option to market the product is not given to the producer; in other cases the financial responsibility is made precise but deemed to be too high by the producer. In both these situations, the producer has to await a clearing decision by the authorities before the product can be marketed, or he simply decides not to produce the product at all. Or when a deposit is specified, he may find that he has sufficient information about his product to assume the financial responsibility and to market the product now instead of after the product

[7] Or this instrument may be used to facilitate harmonization of rules between jurisdictions. In the European community, for example, there are attempts to achieve harmonization among the member countries. Thus in a preliminary program for consumer protection policy it is said that "certain categories of new products which may prejudicially affect the health or safety of consumers should be made subject to special authorization procedures harmonized throughout the Community" (see CED, *Consumer Protection,* p. 65).

has been cleared. In such cases, the producer will be refunded when the product is cleared or when the product is no longer in use in a way that has been specified in advance.

This form of producer liability can be extended beyond physical effects of products on personal and environmental safety. It can cover also selling statements or promises made by the producer in advertising, statements that if untrue merely make the consumer believe that he has wasted his money. In a growing number of countries, there are now consumer protection laws against deceptive advertising (unrelated to personal injury and environmental hazard). In some of these cases, firms have to be proved wrong before they can be stopped from using the contested arguments in the marketing efforts. Or once they have marketed the product, the law can require them to prove they are right (as is the case in Sweden, for example). In either case, some damage to consumers may arise before any action can be taken. If, instead, producers were made financially responsible for making claims not yet proved to be correct by having to make a deposit payment determined by court, consumers could be given an explicit right to protection by compensation. A likely effect, however, is that the firm would abstain from deceptive marketing practices and use only statements that can be proved to be correct. When the proof has been established, the deposit is returned to the firm.

In the case of safety requirements and, in particular, in the case of consumer protection against deceptive advertising, the determination of deposits would not be a simple matter. As we see below, this may be one of the reasons for choosing an alternative to the cash version of the deposit–refund sytem. But the difficulty in finding the appropriate deposit rates is no less a sufficient argument against deposit–refund systems in these applications than in the deposit–refund system discussed earlier that involved measuring environmental effects and similar problems. But more important to note is that the disadvantages of excessive deposits are limited because the amount is refunded when the requirements are met. And when they are not met, the deposits are to be used only to the extent of the estimated damages determined by the courts. Thus the costs of excessive deposits will be limited to some loss of interest. This price as well as the policy costs and other costs (to be discussed in the next section) inherent in the system will have to be weighed against the benefits of the deposit–refund system, that is, the benefits of some "good" products appearing earlier than otherwise, some "bad" products being redesigned or never marketed, "incorrect" selling arguments being avoided, and consumers being protected by compensation against physical harm or deception.

EFFECTS OF PRODUCER LIABILITY
THROUGH DEPOSIT–REFUND SYSTEMS

In the preceding section we discussed a number of new applications of deposit–refund systems. They were designed to (1) protect the value of guarantees or other producer commitments after bankruptcy, (2) protect consumers against products that would have caused personal injury or environmental hazards and against deceptive advertising, (3) provide availability of new products at an earlier date, and (4) protect consumers through compensation in cases of injury, reduced environmental quality, and losses from products bought under false advertising. The introduction of deposit–refund systems for such purposes may affect demand as well as the availability of product supply at a given date. In this section we discuss how cash deposits made by producers who sell products under such systems will affect costs, output, price, product quality, and government revenue. In the next section, we turn to the effects of replacing cash deposits with other arrangements.

In most cases it will be appropriate to have a flat rate of deposits per unit sold. In principle, this rate should reflect the value of maximum producer liability as well as the length of the period (T) during which the commitment is valid. Except for cases of producer-initiated commitments, this period will have been made precise by court rulings or decisions made by the government agency in charge. Up to the date at which the deposit is refunded (in actual fact, of course, it may replace deposits for new units produced), the government owns the deposit. However, the purpose of the deposit does not require that the rate of interest r_g earned on the deposit fund accrues to the government except, perhaps, to cover costs for fund administration. Thus, given that the interest r_g is the property of the depositor, his real cost is determined by the difference between his alternative rate of return on these funds, r_F, and r_g. Because r_F is the rate of return on his preferred type of holdings, we take the difference $r_F - r_g$ in general to be positive. With product quality unchanged and the deposit per unit of output equal to D, we have the addition to unit/costs as at least equal to

$$\Delta C_F = \int_0^T (r_F - r_g) \, De^{-r_F t} \, dt$$

This minimum level of cost increase is the appropriate estimate only when the producer *knows* that the requirements for a refund will be fulfilled. If not, part of the deposit may not be returned. In the bankruptcy case, this will be of interest only to the firm's creditors. But in the case of deposits pending government or court approval of contested product properties, legitimate claims on the firm's deposits would imply a future loss to the firm itself. Let us denote the present value of the expected loss from claims approved by court by a discounted sum of probabilities of loss $P(L)$ of the deposit as a whole, that is, by $P(L)D$ per unit of output. The profit function of the firm before the new deposit system has been introduced is

$$\Pi_A = (b - aX)X - C_F X$$

which includes, if relevant, an ordinary, prebankruptcy, guarantee system. (This system would have affected b by an addition of e_G, and C_F by an addition of $-S_g(V - R)$; see page 37.[8]) If we disregard risk aversion, the new profit function can be written as

$$\Pi_P = (b - aX + e_A)X - (C_F + \Delta C_F)X - P(L)DX \qquad (4\text{-}1)$$

Here e_A is the addition to demand price by the added benefits to consumers (if relevant) as revealed by their market behavior. Thus $e_A \geq 0$, $\Delta C_F > 0$, and $1 > P(L) \geq 0$.

Maximizing Π_P with respect to output, optimal output is

$$X_P = \frac{b - C_F}{2a} + \frac{e_A - \Delta C_F - P(L)D}{2a}$$

X_P is greater than X_A only if $e_A - \Delta C_F - P(L)D > 0$, that is, only if the demand effect is positive and cost effects are insignificant ($r_F \approx r_G$ and $P(L) \approx 0$). With an insignificant effect on demand, output is likely to fall. The same is true for profit, of course. Price, however, is certain to increase as $P_A = (b + C_F)/2$ and

$$p_P = \frac{b + C_F}{2} + \frac{e_A + \Delta C_F + P(L)D}{2}$$

that is, as costs and possibly also demand increase. (In the case of deposits paid for a new product that otherwise would not have existed because of

[8] As before, the symbols used here have the following meaning: $X =$ output, $b - aX =$ a linear price function, $e_G =$ the positive demand effect of a guarantee system, $S_G =$ the fraction of the products that are returned, $V =$ reuse value, and $R =$ refund.

government regulations on product safety, the comparison just made would have no meaning.)

The introduction of this deposit–refund system will affect incentives to change product quality. Take the special case in which quality change does not affect the quality of services that the product offers consumers, aside from the quality aspects connected with the guarantee (assuming that consumers always will be fully compensated under contingencies covered by the deposit–refund system). Here it may pay the producer to undertake product changes at the expense of production cost increases. As follows from equation (4-1), this is profitable up to the point at which

$$\frac{\partial \Pi_P}{\partial C_F} = \left[\frac{de_A}{dC_F} - \frac{d\Delta C_F}{dC_F} - \frac{dP(L)}{dC_F} D - \frac{dD}{dC_F} - 1 \right] X = 0$$

As follows from this expression, product changes may affect factors underlying the deposit rate D and hence reduce ΔC_F and the expected loss $P(L)D$ (by reducing the guarantee, if permitted, or reducing the costs of a given performance guarantee, or in the contested-product-property case, by reducing properties considered to be particularly risky for human beings or the environment). Similar changes, where applicable, could reduce $P(L)$ or T, the latter factor reducing ΔC_F. In addition, all these product changes could influence demand so that $de_A/dC_F \gtrless 0$. Thus changes that would benefit the producer may in some instances hurt consumers.

In the deposit–refund systems discussed in the preceding chapter, deposits have the function of billing social costs to economic agents; here the deposits fulfill a pure insurance function. Therefore requiring deposit payments has, in general, no effects on the government budget or on taxpayers, except for those instances in which deposits replace government expenditure as compensation to groups hurt by unfulfilled guarantees or contracts and by products having detrimental effects on human health or the environment. Such compensatory payments are likely to have been made on an *ad hoc* basis or in a more or less stochastic manner because there are few predetermined and clear rules for when and how such compensations should be made. Hence there would be no precise effects on government expenditure or on taxpayers to take into account, although the actual amounts in specific cases may be quite substantial.

In particular with reference to these more or less arbitrary effects of government behavior as well as to the possible effects on product quality, it is hard to make an overall evaluation of the effects of introducing deposit–refund systems of the type dealt with here. Even if the only effects were that prices increased for an extension of guarantees to cover situations of business failure or prices increased to include an insurance premium for unforeseen compensation requirements, it would be hard to evaluate the change with the ordinary tools of economic analysis. The reason is that there is no market test to be relied upon here. The comparison essentially involves two alternatives with different sets of commodities (with or without a certain extension of a guarantee, with or without a potential compensation device, and so on). In addition, the setting is one of imperfect information; that is, consumers do not know the probabilities of business failure, future detection of product hazards, and so on. With imperfect information and with a comparison of different commodities, standard economic theory has little to say. The same is true, of course, for alternative policy measures reducing the extent of product hazards, the number of guarantees that do not guarantee, and the extent of deceptive sales promotion—that is, alternatives such as outright bans or other purely regulatory means. What we can say about the deposit–refund system, in contrast to these alternatives, is that it introduces a shift in liability of a kind that creates economic incentives for the party that normally has a monopoly on the best available information about risks of bankruptcy and about product properties, that is, the producer. These incentives bear upon the choice of product qualities and producer commitments, with a larger part of the burden of the effects of these changes being placed on the producers instead of the consumers.

Although policy actions of this kind must be based on specific policy goals and hence cannot be derived from the premise of a general goal such as efficiency, economic analysis still has a constructive role to play. If an incentive scheme such as the deposit–refund system is chosen, there are different versions·of this system to be evaluated. So far we have assumed that deposits actually have to be paid by the producer within a field covered by a deposit–refund system. We now investigate the case in which the protection provided by a cash deposit is secured by other means.

SUBSTITUTES FOR CASH DEPOSITS

In all deposit–refund systems it is possible in principle to avoid having deposits affect the liquidity position of the depositor by their full amount. The basis for this argument is that the prospect of a refund constitutes an addition to the gross wealth of the owner of the refundable commodity or contract, which thus improves his borrowing capacity. It is obvious, however, that small deposit amounts, high transactions costs, and uncertainty concerning whether the owner will fulfill the requirements for a refund contribute to making refund prospects unattractive collateral for credit institutions. Therefore borrowing to finance deposits paid by consumers and small firms would seldom be done.

When the deposit amounts increase and the self-interest of the depositor is clearly in favor of meeting the requirements for refunds, both demand for credit and supply of credit for deposit payments will rise. If, in addition, the prospective debtor is already operating in the credit market, transaction costs for the debtor as well as the creditor are likely to be small. Hence we may expect that most of the deposit payments under the deposit–refund system discussed in this chapter as well as substantial producer-paid deposits in general will be covered by credit transactions, that is, by increased borrowing or reduced lending on the part of the depositor. In more formal terms, if r_F—the opportunity capital costs of the deposit—is minimized by credit transactions offered by the credit market, increases in net borrowing will result instead of reductions in liquidity or producer expenditure in the amount of deposits paid, or both.

To the extent that the minimum r_F varies among firms, the deposit–refund system can be seen to have a discriminatory effect on different producers. This may be due to differences in the rate of return on the firm's assets or the interest rate of borrowed funds, the latter of which may in turn be due to differences in debt position or firm size. But the discriminatory effect may change when we consider the alternative of selling the deposit–refund package to a third party, an alternative that is assumed to be chosen if the effect on profits is positive. This would occur if r_F is minimized by this alternative, when r_F is the only cost of the deposit–refund system for the firm, or if $\Delta C_F + P(L)D$ is minimized, when the expected value of a refund loss also affects the producer (see equation (4-1)).

To sell the deposit–refund package to a third party, which takes over the liability of the producer under the deposit–refund system or parts of it, would be acceptable to the government as a substitute for a given deposit payment if there is no risk that the new holder will not fulfill the payment obligation involved. Thus the government could authorize certain institutions to replace the deposit payment of the producer by an equivalent commitment on the part of the institutions. Such institutions we take to be banks or insurance companies.

A possible effect of this kind of liability transfer would seem to be the emergence of a moral hazard. That is to say, the incentives of the deposit–refund system in support of "good" producer behavior might disappear once someone else has taken over the responsibility. This may be a problem when a firm is not interested in being able to buy this kind of service for any longer period of time. In other words, if the producer does not want the same arrangement with any bank or insurance company for "next year's output," it could try to beat the system this year by turning out a low-quality product or by not meeting its obligations to consumers, in a way that would fool a guarantor when the deal is made. But, firms interested in staying in business and in having favorable interest rates offered to them in the future will still have an incentive to produce high-quality products and to meet their commitments. Moreover, producers of the hit-and-run type discussed earlier will probably not succeed very often in getting a bank or an insurance company to offer any guarantee at all or an interest rate sufficiently low to make the producers willing to take the bid. These observations underline what we have already pointed out, namely, that market transactions of liability are likely to be relevant only for large and well-established firms.

The operation of this market for risk taking would run as follows. A producer facing the option of selling a product under the liability determined by a deposit–refund system for extended product guarantees, unknown product hazards, insured restoration of production sites, and so on, with a deposit (normally) per unit of product determined by court or a government agency, approaches an institution authorized to sell contingent payment guarantees. This agent makes ordinary insurance computations for parts or all of the risks involved, with maximum payment liability equal to the deposit requirement, and offers an "insurance premium" to the producer. The producer may or may not take the bid; if not, the producer may prefer to enter the deposit–refund system on its own or abandon the production project in question.

There are several reasons why there would be transactions in an insurance market of this kind. Institutions specializing in these insurance policies (or bank guarantees) may estimate the maximum loss to be lower than the deposit. In fact, costs will refer to expected payments rather than maximum liability. This is one reason why costs for the policy could be lower than costs of making the deposit. Another reason is that the risks for different policy holders will be partly or completely uncorrelated, so that the institution can benefit from risk pooling in a way that the producer cannot. To the extent that moral hazard can be avoided or excluded from the policy coverage, paying the insurance premium is likely to be more attractive to the producer than accepting the cost of deposit payments. This is particularly true if the producer conveys all his information on the risks involved, in support of a low premium. It may not be in the interest of the producer to make all information available to the court or agency that determines the deposit and that must be assumed to be open to public supervision.

The introduction of the insurance substitute for deposit payments will increase overall efficiency in the economy by reducing costs of deposit–refund systems to producers without increasing costs for any other party. In addition, however, efficiency may be improved further by the fact that the courts or agencies determining the deposit rates may now be allowed to make more approximate calculations than without the insurance alternative. The reason is that loose calculations leading to high "safety first" deposit rates, which would be a definite problem when firms are to pay the deposit, are less of an obstacle when the insurer makes his own risk estimates. Thus policy costs may be reduced by extending the deposit–refund system in the way discussed here.

In the next chapter we look into an actual application of a deposit–refund system of this kind. In the remainder of the present chapter we turn to a possible application of deposit–refund systems in the public sector. Here deposit payments are superfluous for obvious reasons; the existence of a government obligation to make compensatory payments must be sufficient when compensation is required by the rules of the system. Thus from an analytical viewpoint, this application would represent an extreme version of the deposit–refund system discussed in this section and would represent the opposite extreme to the case in which individual consumers are forced to make advance payments in cash for obligations imposed on them by government.

DEPOSIT–REFUND SYSTEMS FOR LOWER-LEVEL GOVERNMENT BODIES

Incentives in the government sector constitute a problem in most economies regardless of how mixed they are. Rarely are any economic incentives used for government decision units as a whole, although some such incentives may exist at least implicitly for individual decision makers within a unit indirectly affecting the performance of the unit as a whole.[9] There are, however, incentive system designs that could work in a way similar to those for decision units outside the public sector, that is, for consumers and firms. Such systems are often applicable only to parts of the activities of the agency or department within the federal, state, or local government. Well-known examples of rules for decision making that aim at efficiency and effectiveness are planning-programming-budgeting systems, cost–benefit analysis, and cost–effectiveness analysis. Such instruments may not include economic incentive mechanisms for the government unit in the sense that the actual outcome directly affects the unit's revenue or the budget allocated to the unit. Here we discuss an economic incentive system that has this effect and that may be applicable to parts of the government sector. What it amounts to is a deposit–refund system in the form of financial liability toward consumers of certain public services. To discuss this particular application in more detail would require an extensive analysis of the institutions and the decision-making process of the government sector, which—in addition to being of peripheral interest to our main theme—would, to a large extent, require a separate treatment of individual countries. Therefore we here bring forth only the principal aspects of the possible use of deposit–refund systems inside the public sector.

Let us assume that the top-level government administration (the legislative or the executive branch) views services demanded by consumers or firms and produced by individual government agencies or local governments as in principle similar to services produced by private firms. Then the incentive structure that is "sanctioned," "accepted," or "prescribed" for the private sector—established by the fact that the government has not intervened in or at least not eliminated the fundamental parts of this structure—may prove to be a useful instrument to promote efficiency in the government sector as well. Government services for which this view seems possible include permits, licenses, patent rights, and similar decisions by authorities where delays would have a detrimental effect on the consumer or producer applicant. Services from government-operated activities could also be included, such as highway construction, public transportation facilities, and schools, where delays may arise in a predetermined time schedule or where reversals of gov-

---

[9] See, for example, the bonus plan proposed by President Carter in 1978. This plan would under certain performance criteria provide bonus payments to higher public officials.

ernment decisions may occur concerning master plans, supply of services produced by government, and so on, that authorities previously had decided would hold for at least a certain time period.

The introduction of an incentive mechanism in this context presupposes that a top-level government body has laid down certain principles for how activities like the ones just mentioned should be run. Such rules could spell out that applications for permits and licenses should be processed in a given maximum time, that construction of highways should be completed before a given deadline, and that decisions with respect to master plans and supply of services should have a minimum length of duration.[10] It is not to be assumed that the top-level government body would like to introduce stringent principles of this kind when uncertainty puts a premium on flexibility. But in many cases it is conceivable that the government regards as inefficient or unfair those costs that are imposed on individual consumers and producers because of an absence of a firm commitment as to a maximum or minimum date of delivery or because of a deviation from such time limits. The existence of a formal system of time limits and—to highlight the incentive mechanism in question—economic liability on the responsible agency or local government body could in such cases act as a safeguard against excessive external costs and as a facility for compensation of the remaining damages to firms and individual persons.

The question may be asked to what extent the imposition of a financial liability on an individual agency or local government in fact would promote efficiency. If the deadlines were broken and a predetermined compensation were to be paid to the affected party, the effect on the government unit would be not a reduction in "profits"—which would be the result with a private producer—but, typically, a reduction in its activities. In other words, the operations for which the unit has been given financial

---

[10] An example showing that governments in fact may like to establish time limits on the activities of low-level government bodies can be found in the U.S. Consumer Product Safety Act. This act prescribes that safety standards should be developed by a special *ad hoc* committee (manned by people outside government but organized by the Consumer Product Safety Commission (CPSC)) within 150 days and that the proposal made by this committee should be reviewed by CPSC within 60 days. It may be noted in passing that these time limits have been exceeded in four out of five major cases (according to *The Washington Post,* February 25, 1978) possibly because of the absence of a system to enforce these rules. Thus, instead of meeting the 150/60 day requirement, action was completed for TV receivers in 413/484 days, for book matches in 100/524 days, for power lawn mowers in 290/657, and for architectural glass in 171/383 days.

means must be reduced in comparison with what otherwise would have been the case. Such a reduction in operations or in the growth of operations would of course have detrimental effects on the public that is supposed to be served. Thus, in contrast to applications of producer liability in the private sector, it is not the decision makers but the third-party individuals or firms that are punished. Moreover, to assume an unwillingness of the unit to break deadlines and so on and hence an increased likelihood of greater reliability of the services produced by the unit presupposes that the unit "cares" about what happens to its future scale of operations. If it does not care as private producers are assumed to care about reduced profits, there would not be any incentive for increased reliability or efficiency from this system.

Having said this, we must recall the basis from which we started—the difficulty of finding any incentive system that promotes efficiency in the government sector. In contrast to a competitive private sector, there is no exit option for customers. The government has a monopoly, and thus customers cannot turn to competitors or, in many cases, to any other service similar to the one demanded. Or, whenever a shift to another (local) government is considered to be an alternative, the exit option may be formal only, given that the applicant often demands a one-time service and does not know its quality until it is too late to choose a substitute. What remains in the conventional paradigm of customer protest then is the "voice" option. But the reason that efficiency in parts of the government sector is a problem at all is because voices are not heard or for some other reason have not been effective. Thus, if efficiency remains a problem after possible exit and voice options have been tried, we have to turn to other instruments and make a trade-off given that they are not likely to be flawless. What the instrument discussed here may accomplish in this perspective is more fuss about government "malpractice" and more trouble for the individual decision maker, both of which are likely to improve performance in the government sector.

In addition to recalling these particular characteristics of the public sector, we must point out that there are instances in which economic incentives in fact may play a significant role for decision making in this sector. In certain socialist countries such as the German Democratic Republic and Hungary, firms have been subjected to effluent charges although such measures would seem to amount to nothing more than an "intragovernmental transfer" in these cases. But once such charges are allowed to influence something that is cherished by those working in the firm, these economic instruments are likely to have an incentive effect.

In the cases just mentioned, the charges are said to influence the volume of fringe benefits given to the management and the employees.[11] Thus an incentive effect is obviously likely to arise. But this would be true also for a government bureaucracy in a capitalist country where the government tries to maximize the size of the operations of the unit and hence the size of its budget.[12]

Given the demand for incentive mechanisms in the government sector as well as the sensitivity to economic incentives that actually may exist in this sector, there is a potential role for a deposit–refund system here, too. Assume that the presence of financial liability toward the "customers" of a government unit in fact would make it reduce slacks and increase its efforts to avoid breaking deadlines. That, however, may not be an altogether beneficial result. If the unit meets deadlines by making hasty decisions or in other ways reducing "product quality," the net outcome may be negative. Thus we may establish a set of conditions that have to be met to make sure that efficiency improvements would follow from the introduction of financial liability on a low-level government unit: (1) that there are facilities for outside quality control of the output, (2) that financial liability affects behavior and the organization of production so that slacks are reduced, and (3) that there are either alternative sources of finance such as fees or local taxes or the possibility of *ad hoc* additional funds from high-level government, if liabilities actually lead to payments *and* a local government or the high-level government wants to avoid some of the effects of payments on the subsequent scale of production. To avoid contradiction with the incentive assumption under condition (2), this condition (3) would obviously require that alternative sources of finance are more expensive or troublesome for the (local) unit and that additional funds allotted by the government to the unit are determined from case to case after payments actually have been made.[13]

[11] I am indebted to Karl-Göran Mäler for this piece of information.

[12] See, for example, William A. Niskanen, *Bureaucracy and Representative Government* (Chicago, Aldine, 1971).

[13] An illustration, although rather special, of a case in which these conditions seem to be fulfilled and the introduction of financial liability for a government unit is expected to increase efficiency can be taken from the academic world (!). At Stockholm University (state-owned), publishing costs for dissertations are covered by government funds (up to a point), regardless of whether the dissertation is accepted or not. The outcome is determined by a multidisciplinary committee on which representatives of the Ph.D. candidate's discipline constitute a minority. After a series of allegedly low-quality dissertations were produced, it was proposed that the host department for the dissertation should pay 50 percent of publishing costs if the dissertation were not accepted—unless the department had not told the

If, for a group of low-level government units, these conditions are satisfied sufficiently for an improved performance to occur, the introduction of financial liability for these units may be worthwhile on efficiency grounds alone. It should be borne in mind, however, that the liability instrument has effects other than efficiency effects and that these other effects may be even more important. Financial liability as suggested here would mean that it is possible and straightforward to compensate the party actually hurt by the government unit breaking the rules that have been set up for it. If such compensations are enacted, the negative effects of uncertainty of government planning and government operations would no longer be borne only or at all by the "customers" who bear no responsibility for the outcome. In other words, certain undesirable distributional effects that otherwise might occur are reduced by the liability system.

It should be observed that if the government wants to have compensations paid out for negative effects of certain forms of government activity, there are in fact two alternative ways in which such compensations could be accomplished. Either the compensatory responsibility stays with the unit in charge of the activity in question, as we have been assuming so far, or it is placed on the government sector as a whole, for example, on a special unit making compensatory payments from the general budget according to decisions by courts. The difference between these two alternatives is of course that the unit in charge of production bears direct and formal financial responsibility for its actions only in the former case. In addition, flexibility is higher in this case, where top-level government may choose *ad hoc* to take over the financial burden *ex post facto*.

At first glance it may look as if we have now moved a considerable distance from the deposit–refund systems discussed in earlier sections. In conclusion, it may be appropriate to once again make conspicuous the link that exists here.

We started out by analyzing cases in which we could not be sure that individual private agents would fulfill existing commitments, that is, make deliveries as specified or pay compensation for not doing so, and cases in which policy costs for eliminating such uncertainty were prohibitively high. In the pursuit of some policy goal such as efficiency, the government

---

candidate in writing to abstain from presenting his dissertation. Given the limited room for luxury spending by Swedish university departments, the effect is likely to be a halt to the presentation of low-quality dissertations and, perhaps, a delay for some medium-quality dissertations as well.

might want such agents to make prepayments (deposits) and offer them conditional return payments (refunds). Shifting to firms and organizations of an increasing size and stability, we tended to move up the ladder of solvency and of certainty of meeting long-term commitments and down the ladder of policy costs. Thus it became increasingly likely that prepayments would not be called for either because special institutions would emerge to take over the obligations involved and provide full (or sufficient) certainty at a competitive price or because the agent itself could provide such a degree of certainty. This final stage was arrived at when agents inside the government sector were forced to take on certain commitments that, although they are attached to goods and services that are different from those provided by the private sector, have impacts on consumers and private producers of the same general nature ("guaranteed satisfaction or money back"). Throughout this spectrum of different agents and different kinds of commodities, the deposit–refund system in its original or its "degenerate" versions provides mechanisms for compensation and for economic incentives to reduce wasteful use of scarce resources.

SUMMARY

In this chapter we have discussed the possible use of deposit–refund systems to create or extend guarantees of product performance where existing performance bonds provided by the market economy and by existing laws appear to be insufficient in view of a certain set of government policy goals. Such goals are primarily in the area of consumer policy, though this policy should then be interpreted in a broad sense to include also indirect effects on consumers and effects on services supplied to producers.

In the first sections of this chapter, we saw how financial liability introduced through a deposit–refund system could be used to secure the operation of market-generated or government-initiated forms of delivery contracts as well as guarantees concerning the functioning of commodities, the disposal of used products, and the restoration of production sites under conditions of bankruptcy of the guarantor. We also discussed how a similar system could be used to support the viability of guarantees introduced to protect against certain undesirable effects of new commodities and, possibly, certain questionable marketing and sales promotion

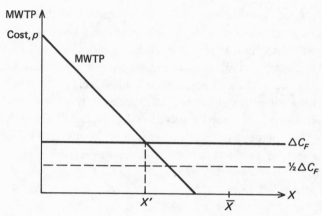

Figure 4-1.

activities by firms. Such applications of deposit–refund systems that involve payments by producers would, however, be likely to deviate from the deposit–refund systems for consumers discussed earlier in that a market for buying substitutes for cash deposits (from banks, for example) would or could be established. Moreover, such a market could be seen to improve the overall efficiency of the deposit–refund system.

The effects of producer-paid deposit–refund systems would in general imply cost increases for producers and hence price increases for the commodities involved. In addition, incentives calling for extensive changes in product quality could arise. To some extent the system could replace certain *ad hoc* government expenditure that now exists. The probable net effect on producer profits would in many cases be negative, although tendencies for demand to increase as a consequence of the consumer benefits provided by the deposit–refund system would mitigate and possibly outweigh the effects of increased costs on profits. Moreover, in the special cases in which the deposit–refund system would allow new products to be marketed at an earlier date than otherwise, there could be clear net advantages to producers.

Part of the effects on consumers is illustrated by the use of figure 4-1. The MWTP curve shows the marginal aggregate willingness to pay for an extension or introduction of a guarantee of an existing unchanged product. $\bar{X}$ indicates the volume of this unchanged product that would otherwise be bought. With the new guarantee, average and marginal costs would increase by ΔC_F. If prices (say, on a competitive market) increased by this amount, consumers of quantities up to X' would win, if we disregard secondary effects of the system. Consumers of units $\bar{X} - X'$ would lose, unless the market still provided the alternative of the commodity at the old guarantee level and at the old price. (In a simple linear monopoly case, a cost increase of ΔC_F would lead to a price increase of $1/2\ \Delta C_F$, if demand did not rise, and by more than this if demand did rise.)

In more general terms, consumers would benefit from the (extended) guarantee in that this institutional change would (1) create incentives that tend to reduce uncertainty as to the implications of contracts and guarantees or reduce the number of commodities with negative effects on health and the environment or commodities sold with incorrect advertising, and (2) provide funds for compensation in cases of damage under these conditions. This might benefit in particular consumers with a low information capacity. But the net distributional effects, after the actual price effects are taken into account, would have to be analyzed for each separate case.

In the preceding section of this chapter, we discussed a counterpart of the deposit–refund system for the private sector that could resolve certain efficiency problems in the public sector as well as certain compensation problems that the government might acknowledge here. This counterpart would be a financial liability system for individual low-level government bodies concerning certain public services such as delivery of permits or licenses within specified time limits or the availability of public transportation (specified) for certain time periods. Potential drawbacks of this application of the deposit–refund system include possibly very small effects on incentives and undesirable effects on quality and future supply of these services. But in spite of these possible drawbacks and in particular, of course, in cases in which these drawbacks do not appear, the advantages in terms of more reliable commitments concerning delivery dates, incentives to reduce slacks, and the facilities for compensation of consumers and producers affected could be strong enough to justify the use of a version of a deposit–refund system in parts of the public sector. The political choice to be made here depends, however, on the specific "consumer policy" goals of the government and, in particular, on the extent to which economic incentives and compensatory institutions are allowed to play a role in this context. Although financial liability placed on a government unit may not have the same direct effect as that which is placed on a private, profit-maximizing firm, it may have strong indirect effects on decision makers and thus provide a valuable stimulus to efficiency in parts of the public sector.

5 THE EMPIRICAL EVIDENCE

INTRODUCTION

The theoretical analysis in the preceding chapters contains a series of suggested applications of deposit–refund systems. The success of such applications depends, of course, on actual circumstances in each specific case and country. Nevertheless, it would have been valuable if we could have extended the analysis by indicating the costs and benefits of introducing deposit–refund systems in certain key areas, at least by estimating probable orders of magnitude of the crucial variables involved. One attempt of this sort is made in the final chapter. But, such *ex ante* investigations provide little insight into the adjustment process and the probable long-run effects of a deposit–refund system. These adjustments and effects can be expected to be considerable, given that the application in question has not been made before. For that reason, in particular, it is interesting to look more closely at those areas where deposit–refund systems actually have been applied. Such applications, however special they may seem, could suggest market reactions, administrative difficulties, and so on, of a nature common to all or most potential deposit–refund systems. But, in addition, investigations into actual applications of deposit–refund systems in a particular region or country may be interesting in themselves, as a guide to future policy in the markets concerned.

98

It seems almost impossible to sound too many warnings about the uncertainty surrounding empirical studies and about the risks of being misled by available figures. Already in the special area of beverage container deposits, on which so many studies have been carried out lately, the uncertainties of the available evidence are impressive. This is made obvious by the many diverging evaluations and conclusions that these studies provide—a particular benefit of repeated empirical investigations. Moreover, the outcome of particular applications may be dominated by special policy choices made and by the time periods that the analysis covers. Therefore we cannot expect too much by way of precision from the available evidence.

An important piece of evidence is that deposit–refund systems in fact have been operating over long periods. Market-generated refund systems have passed a minimum test of producer profitability and consumer acceptance. These applications cover not only various containers and transportation facilities but also the rental market in general, product warranties, protective clauses in contracts concerning services offered, and so on. In addition, the past record of scrap markets and secondhand markets contains ingredients that would be relevant for an evaluation of deposit–refund systems.

Unfortunately, few studies of market-generated systems seem to have been undertaken or made public. As for specific government-initiated systems, applications have been limited to a few markets and a few regions. In addition, there are problems in interpreting the studies that exist.

How can an improvement in the state of empirical knowledge be achieved? Aside from the "spontaneous" growth of deposit–refund systems in the future and the spontaneous curiosity about what they actually will have accomplished, the basic potential source of information would seem to be found in experimental introduction of government-initiated systems carefully prepared for evaluation studies. A persistent problem, in view of information and evaluation, seems to be that governments often make decisions on the basis of *a priori* analyses in the spirit of final, "best-of-all-worlds," decisions. When the unexpected flaws and disadvantages of the chosen path appear, there may be limited possibilities for a many-sided evaluation and for adequate adjustments, if a system of program control has not been introduced to begin with or if a period of controlled experiments has not been admitted. This is not to say that an experimental approach to policy change would be a guarantee against misinformation; experiments have their pitfalls in terms of uncertainty about Hawthorne effects (effects particular to the experimental setting), the influence of vested interests, and whether the extent and duration of these tests are sufficient. But, given the definite shortage of this kind of empirical evidence at the present time, more of it would be a worthwhile investment. This seems to be a relevant hypothesis, particularly for policy areas such as those discussed here, where—given the uncertainty—full-scale policy changes are made slowly, after long periods of *a priori* deliberations.

We now turn to look at some of the empirical evidence on deposit–refund systems that is available. First, we summarize the main variables emerging from the preceding analysis. Next, we compare this list with some of the results presented in studies of government-initiated systems, most of which refer to beverage container deposits during recent years. We also look at applications to waste lubrication oil, auto hulks, and charter flight packages in several countries.

INFORMATION NEEDS

In the theoretical analysis of the preceding chapters, we began with the case of *producer-initiated refund systems*. Information about such systems would be useful for designing government-initiated systems in other areas. In addition and more directly, this kind of information would be of great help for government intervention in established refund systems, wherever such actions are called for.

The most desirable data about market-generated systems are perhaps the *value of returned products* (V), which in many cases would be known by the producer, and the *disposal costs* for returns (C_R) and disposal costs for dumping (C_d), which may have been studied by the producer. The disposal costs are of course possible to analyze without cooperation from the producers involved. Here it would be interesting to know what determines the levels of C_R and C_d as well as how these costs tend to vary among consumer groups, stratified with respect to income, location variables, storage space, access to a car, refuse collection facilities, billing principles, and so on. Moreover, it would be desirable to know what effects refund offers (and offers to accept returns without a refund) have had on the choice of disposal alternative, that is, the *portion of products returned* (gR). For durable goods, we would also be interested in the *effect on disposal dates,* given that the refund offer may affect the period during which a product is used or just kept in storage. Aside from the effects on disposal activities, we would like to know how a refund offer affects *demand* for the product (to determine e, see equation (2-1) in chapter 2). If the demand function with respect to price were known, this additional piece of information would make it possible to translate a given refund offer into a change in prices. Under ideal circumstances, we could also obtain estimates of the resulting effects on equilibrium *prices and output* in the short run versus the long run.

Finally, it would be of particular interest to know what *administrative costs* refund systems of various kinds entail for the firms as well as what administrative technology is used and has been attempted. Because the administrative aspect could be crucial to the efficiency of government-initiated systems, such data would be valuable.

Turning to *deposit–refund systems* actually introduced by government and to other government sources of information relevant for applications of such systems, we first ask for data on *the social benefits* (A) achieved by product returns as compared with alternative forms of disposal. Thus we are interested in estimates of the effects of environmental degradation, littering, and other improper ways of disposal that are avoided by product returns. Moreover, data on energy savings and material recovery are desirable when such resources are underpriced in the market. And it would be valuable to have at least rough estimates of consumer benefits from government-initiated warranty systems and similar deposit–refund systems. In addition, short-run and long-run estimates of the *market value of returned products* (V), that is, the reuse or scrap value, would be of great interest. And, in particular, it would be interesting to obtain information about the extent to which these values are passed on to consumers by a process of competition in the reprocessing market (see page 55).

Again, data on *disposal costs* (C_R and C_d or the $C_R - C_d$ difference) and their variation among consumer groups are of crucial importance, as are estimates of propensities to return used products (PR) as functions of the refund rate (see figure 3-4). In particular applications of deposit–refund systems, the activities of scavengers or "free-lance" collectors of used products may be important to single out. And especially for the "incentive-reinforcement" case, it is of interest to know the actual adjustments in PR functions over time (see figure 3-2).

As was the case for market-generated systems, we would like to know the *demand effects* ($\bar{e}$, e') (see equation [3-1]) and *price effects* of

government-sponsored systems. In addition, deposit–refund systems have discernible effects on the producer choice of *product design* and technology. Data on such effects as well as estimates of the risks of the appearance of *"pirate" producers* of refundable products would be essential pieces of information.

Government-initiated systems of the tax-subsidy type give rise to a special set of effects that influence the evaluation of such systems. One is the effect on the *budget* of a deposit–refund surplus. Another is the effect on consumers and other deposit-payers in their role of *creditors* with an estimate of the different interest rates involved. Given the policy objective of a government-initiated system, we would also like to have data on alternative policy solutions such as product charges. Here administrative and other *policy costs* of the deposit–refund system and its competitors would play an important role, as would their respective *distributional* effects.

Thus we have identified a long list of information required to evaluate the practical effects of introducing deposit–refund systems. We now compare these desiderata with the available empirical evidence. As we indicated earlier, however, we cannot yet satisfy all of these requirements.

MANDATORY DEPOSITS ON BEVERAGE CONTAINERS

The mandatory deposit on beverage containers seems to be the most widespread actual application of government-initiated deposit–refund systems so far. This field has received particular attention for several reasons. First, beverage containers represent a substantial part of solid waste and of waste treatment costs; they are a major source of littering, and recycling or reuse can save energy.[1] Second, producers and consumers have considerable experience with market-generated deposit systems in this area; thus it has been fairly easy for policy makers to understand how government-initiated systems would work and what the consumer reactions would be.

The empirical evidence from the applications of deposit–refund systems to beverage containers is interesting *per se,* but the relevance of available data can hardly be limited to applications in this particular area. Deposit–

[1] Saving energy may be a policy goal for a government even if energy prices have been adjusted to reflect scarcity.

refund systems would seem to be directly applicable also to other cases in which the buyer purchases many items of a product or class of products over time and the deposit–refund is, absolutely speaking, quite small (such as paper, metals, and other ingredients in waste).

Several summaries and evaluations have been made of the existing studies of beverage container deposits. The presentation in this chapter relies heavily on two of these, the Research Triangle Institute (RTI) study of 1975 and, in particular, the Organization for Economic Cooperation and Development (OECD) study of 1978.[2] We extract findings from these reports to the extent that they bear on the central empirical issues exposed in the preceding section. The reader with special interest in beverage container deposits *per se* is referred to the two studies mentioned, the literature cited therein, and a report by the Resource Conservation Committee.[3]

Background and Motives

In recent years the unregulated market for beverages has tended to shift steadily toward the sale of beverages in nonreturnable containers. The U.S. role as a leader in consumer product development and the limited extent of government intervention in the United States make it particularly relevant to illustrate the market trend with data from this country. Table 5-1 shows the data for beer and soft drinks from 1963 to 1973 and 1977 (forecast). Disregarding the fact that a minor portion of metal cans actually are returned, we see that the portion of the beverages sold in returnable containers has declined from 46 percent to 12 percent for beer and from 89 percent to 38 percent for soft drinks during this fourteen-year period. The trend is similar for other countries with no or minor government intervention.[4]

This tendency of the unregulated beverage container market has put an increased strain on municipal solid waste management and on the receptive capacity of the environment. Beverage containers account for some 2–12 percent of all solid waste (by weight) in the OECD countries;

[2] Research Triangle Institute (RTI), *Energy and Economic Impacts of Mandatory Deposits* (distributed by National Technical Information Service, Springfield, Va., as PB-258-638, 1975); Organization for Economic Cooperation and Development (OECD), *Beverage Containers—Reuse or Recycling* (Paris, 1978).

[3] Resource Conservation Committee, *Committee Findings and Staff Papers on National Beverage Container Deposits* (Washington, D.C., 1979).

[4] OECD, *Beverage Containers,* pp. 21–28.

Table 5-1. Beer and Soft Drinks Sold in the United States from 1963 to 1973, by Container Type
(percentage)

Year	Returnable glass bottles	Nonreturnable glass bottles	Metal cans
Beer			
1963	46	16	38
1964	42	18	40
1965	41	19	40
1966	38	19	43
1967	35	21	44
1968	31	21	48
1969	29	22	49
1970	26	22	52
1971	23	21	56
1972	22	20	58
1973	19	21	60
1977 (forecast)	11	23	66
Soft drinks			
1963	89	3	8
1964	86	4	10
1965	82	5	13
1966	75	8	17
1967	65	13	22
1968	58	15	27
1969	49	21	30
1970	40	27	33
1971	39	27	34
1972	38	28	34
1973	35	29	36
1977 (forecast)	38	26	36

Source: Research Triangle Institute, *Energy and Economic Impacts of Mandatory Deposits* (distributed by National Technical Information Service, Springfield, Va., as PB-258-638, 1975) app. B; and Resource Conservation Committee, *Choices for Conservation* (Washington, D.C., 1977) p. 85.

packaging as a whole accounts for 30–60 percent. Beverage containers represent between 7 and 33 percent of litter by unit count or between 34 and 70 percent by volume according to a number of studies reported in the OECD study. Moreover, in 1972, the U.S. Environmental Protection Agency (EPA) estimated that beverage-related litter was increasing by 8 percent per year in the United States.[5]

[5] Ibid., pp. 11, 49, and 52.

In general, individual units of waste disposal service are not priced; often waste collection (70 percent of costs) and final disposal (30 percent of costs) are not priced at all but financed out of taxes. Thus beverage container waste like other waste does not carry a price tag for the individual corresponding to the marginal social costs of collection and disposal. Because different types of beverage containers have different relative propensities to end up in the waste stream, their effects on waste management costs are not revealed to the consumer. Similarly, the consumer is not billed for littering (except perhaps in areas where littering laws are strictly enforced and fines are used), and, in general, no account is taken of the fact that container types differ as to their propensity to appear in litter.[6] It should be noted, however, that these propensities cannot be expected to remain constant if measures are taken to increase the percentage of returnable containers. Also, returnable containers may be discarded, of course; so, when consumers are "transferred" from one container type to another, they may simply keep their original disposal pattern.

Both the solid waste cost problem and the littering problem, the latter being the collection costs and the external effects of littering imposed on the society, have provided motives for government intervention in the beverage container market. There are other motives as well, primarily energy savings. As we pointed out earlier, a separate motive of this kind presupposes that energy is underpriced or that energy savings represent a merit want. If so, it may be noted that the total energy use varies substantially among different types of containers. Table 5-2 shows the results of a study by RTI for the United States. The data would be somewhat changed if it were taken into account that some 15 percent of the aluminum cans actually are recycled and that the assumed trippage rate[7] of ten, although consistent with return rates in 1975 reported by OECD, may be a little too high when measures are taken to move toward a higher percentage of returnable containers. However, the data presented in table 5-2 are roughly in line with the results of other studies for the United States and countries such as Canada, Germany, and Sweden.

In an attempt to avoid the undesirable effects of nonreturnable beverage containers, deposit–refund systems have been introduced by the government in certain countries, certain states in the United States, and

6 Ibid., pp. 55–58.
7 Trippage is the number of times that a returnable bottle is reused.

Table 5-2. Total Energy Requirements for 100 Litres of Beer and Soft Drinks in 12-oz Containers for the United States in 1975 (therms, 1 therm = 10^5 BTU)

Container type	Beer	Soft drinks
Aluminum can[a]	18.7	18.7
Bimetallic can	12.2	12.3
Nonreturnable glass	11.4	12.0[b]
Returnable glass[c]	5.7	3.6[b]

Source: Research Triangle Institute, *Energy and Economic Impacts of Mandatory Deposits* (distributed by National Technical Information Service, Springfield, Va., as PB-258-638, 1975) as cited in Organization for Economic Cooperation and Development, *Beverage Containers—Reuse or Recycling* (Paris, 1978) pp. 67–72.
[a] 100 percent virgin metal.
[b] 16-oz containers.
[c] Ten trips.

certain provinces in Canada. Two routes can be taken. One is a ban on nonrefundable containers, with deposits to be determined by the market, and the other is a mandatory deposit on all kinds of containers. We now look at available data on variables of crucial importance in such systems.

Data on Relevant Variables

Data on social benefits (A). For obvious reasons, no reliable data are available for the *external effects* of littering, that is, the aesthetic effects and the physical damage to human beings and animals because of broken glass and can ring-tabs, and so on. Because there seems to be wide agreement that the avoidance of such effects is the most important source of benefits from an increased rate of container returns, the determination of the optimal deposit will have to be made without a firm basis of data. Moreover, the evaluation of the deposit–refund system as a whole will have to be made on the basis of estimates of the overall effects excluding the external effects, assuming the remaining effects in fact can be estimated with some accuracy.

The gross social benefits (A) of an increase in container returns have ingredients other than or in addition to the external effects avoided (E). One is the reduction in costs of *waste management.* Available data indicate that this value may be below 1 cent per nonreturnable container. Based on estimates reported in the OECD study, this value may have been of the order of 0.1 cent per 12-oz container for the United States in the early 1970s. Although total savings of waste management costs may be of the order of $100 million (estimated for a complete switch to returnable containers in 1972), it is clear that the waste management savings per container will have a negligible effect on the optimal deposit rate.

Another possible ingredient in the gross social benefit of using a returnable container and actually returning it, instead of using a nonreturnable container and not recovering anything from it, is the *net energy savings* (see table 5-2). The value of such savings would have to be determined by the margin of a shadow price for energy over the market price. No explicit data on such a shadow price (which may vary among governments) seem to be available, however.

Instead of the full external effects of littering, the social costs may be influenced by the *costs of collecting litter (C)*. Some estimates are available here, ranging from 2 cents (in the United States in 1969) to 11 cents (in Sweden in 1975) per littered container.[8] Whenever this source of social benefits from using fewer nonreturnable containers is relevant, it must obviously have an important effect on the optimal deposit rate.

Data on the value of returned products (V). The net value to the recipient of a reusable glass bottle would equal approximately the costs of producing a new returnable bottle minus the costs of handling the returned bottle. This net value was estimated to be some 10 cents per bottle for the United States in 1972.[9] If almost all bottles returned to the producer were deemed to be suitable for reuse, which implies that bottles were primarily taken out of use by being broken by the consumer or for other reasons not returned, this 10 cent figure would be a relevant approximate value of bottles returned (the costs of transportation from retailer to producer being very small). This suggests that refunds or total payments per returned bottle in market-generated systems, which were approximately 5 cents at the time, tend to be set below, perhaps far below, the relevant *V* value.

In the case of containers that can be recycled but not reused, that is, cans and broken glass containers, there are data indicating that the *V* value still is positive. For example, there are companies in the United States paying up to 0.75 cents per aluminum can (1975). Moreover, glass- and

[8] OECD, *Beverage Containers,* p. 52.
[9] Ibid., p. 31.

metal-recycling experiments in Sweden reveal a positive V in terms of a (small) net reduction in solid waste management costs.[10] Other sources seem to indicate yet smaller and in some cases even negative net values, at least when recycling rates are low. In other words, there are indications of scale economies in this field (see the discussion in the introduction to chapter 3).

Data on disposal costs (C_R and C_d). It is obvious that the costs to the consumer of returning beverage containers from household use will tend to exceed the costs of alternative forms of disposal. In the literature, this difference, $C_R - C_d > 0$, is often called the "convenience value" of non-returnable containers. Again, it is difficult to estimate a variable such as this for which individual preferences are likely to play an important role. It is not enough to estimate storage costs and time costs for extra handling in taking the container to the store (and, possibly, first bringing it back from a picnic). A survey study made in Canada in 1974 suggested that 70 percent of the respondents would not be willing to pay 3 cents as a convenience value; that is, their statements implied that $C_R{}^i - C_d{}^i < 3$ cents.

In Oregon, where all beverage containers in 1972 were required to carry a minimum deposit of 5 cents (2 cents for standardized containers) and where certain nonreturnable containers (those with ring-tabs or pull-tabs) were prohibited, there were substantial effects on the propensity to return containers. The market share of returnable bottles increased from 31 percent (beer) and 53 percent (soft drinks) twelve months before the implementation of the bill to 96 percent (beer) and 88 percent (soft drinks) twelve months after the implementation. At the same time, return rates for such bottles increased from 75–80 percent to 90–95 percent. If we disregard the possibility that psychological factors played a role in this pioneer effort to reduce the container problem, the results suggest that deposit rates of 5 cents were enough to exceed the $C_R - C_d$ difference for almost all consumers.

For consumption outside the household, such as in restaurants, the $C_R - C_d$ difference may be expected to be zero or even negative. This discrepancy between on- and off-premise disposal costs is also shown by available estimates of trippage rates. Thus RTI has estimated trippage rates for the United States to be 50 on- and 3 off-premise.[11]

[10] Ibid., pp. 132–133.
[11] Ibid., pp. 87, 109, and 143.

Effects on demand, prices, and output. The effects on prices and output of a mandatory deposit on all containers for beer and soft drinks have been estimated in various studies for the United States. Given that deposits on all containers will be the same as the deposit already existing for returnable containers, only consumers of nonreturnable containers will be directly affected. Some of them will switch to returnable containers whereas others will stay with the nonreturnable containers (predominantly cans) in spite of the fact that these containers are more expensive now. This implies a reduction in demand for nonreturnables and probably an increase of their price due to the smaller turnover; nonreturnables may even disappear, at least from certain local stores. Those who switch will tend to reduce their demand for beverages because their preferred alternative (containers without deposits) has disappeared. Given that the price of the beverage itself remains the same, this group will pay a lower price for the beverage plus the container, provided the container is returned. This is based on the assumption usually made that trippage rates remain high enough for costs of returnable containers to be smaller for the producer than costs of nonreturnable containers. But because average trippage rates can be expected to be reduced by the lower propensity to return containers from this new group of consumers of returnables, prices for beverages in returnable containers would tend to rise. Because those who buy returnables and do not return them will have to pay a higher price for the product they demand, prices will increase for all the products—beverages whose containers are not returned and beverages whose containers are returned. Money outlay per unit of beverage may decline, however, as some consumers switch from nonreturnables to returnables that are in fact returned, given that the new outlay on the latter remains lower than the old outlay on the former. But under the assumption that changes in producer costs are passed on to consumers and with some price elasticity in demand, sales are certain to be reduced.

These deliberations may now be compared with data from specific *ex ante* and *ex post* studies of mandatory deposits. The OECD study reports that most studies carried out for the U.S. government "assume no significant decline in sales as a result of a mandatory 5-cent deposit legislation." In a study of a mandatory system for Illinois, Folk assumes a decline in cost-based prices but no change in consumption.[12] This "price" decline is supposedly a decline in money outlay per unit of beverage,

---

[12] Hugh Folk, *Two Papers on the Effects of Mandatory Deposits on Beverage Containers* (Centre for Advanced Computation, University of Illinois, 1975).

which we showed to be possible above. Similar results are reached in several other U.S. studies; for example, a 0.5-cent decline in total internal costs per 12-oz container of beverage (equal to the average money outlay if passed on to the consumer) is estimated by RTI. Moreover, EPA has estimated the effects of a 10-cent deposit and arrived at an assumed 4 percent decline in sales.[13] A higher deposit will of course tend to reduce demand more, although trippage rates may increase, hence reducing total internal costs per unit of consumption for those returning their containers. (Average trippage rates would increase if consumers, who would have bought returnables already at a lower mandatory deposit, increase their container returns sufficiently to outweigh the effect on trippage rates from those consumers who switch to returnables because of the increase in the mandatory deposit and who can be assumed to have a below-average propensity to return containers.)

In Oregon, consumers are said to "pay slightly less in total for the same volume of beverage than would have been the case under the pre-Bottle Bill conditions." Moreover, it is claimed that "consumption of beverages has not declined as a result of the legislation." As to the combined effects on the operating income of the beverage industry, container manufacturers, distributors, and retailers, there are conflicting views, ranging from a net increase of $3.9 million per year according to one study to a net decrease of $6.9–8.6 million per year according to another. The reason for the discrepancy is the lower return rates used in the latter study.[14]

Evaluation

Some attempts at evaluating the overall effects of mandatory deposits on beer and soft drink containers have been made. Let us look briefly at the Oregon case, which has received most of the attention.

The estimated effects on *littering* were impressive. But, as was suggested above, it may be hard to ascribe these effects to the "all-container deposit" alone, given that this was a pioneering policy effort in a perhaps unusually environment-conscious state. The observed number of beverage containers littered per mile of road per month was reported to have decreased from 127 to 43. Non-beverage-related litter remained un-

[13] OECD, *Beverage Containers*, pp. 101–103.
[14] Ibid., p. 110.

affected. Long-run savings in total solid waste management costs for household waste are estimated to be about 5 percent, due to the reduced volume of beverage-related waste.[15]

Because the return option existed prior to the Bottle Bill, no *beverage consumers* could benefit from the bill (see chapter 3) unless actual prices declined. But as we have seen, prices for each of the various product packages involved are likely to increase. Thus there are only losers to be found among the consumers. The effects on the producer sector as a whole are uncertain, as we just saw, but it seems a bit farfetched to assume that cost increases for the industry and the retail business are not passed on to consumers in the long run. As to the remaining effects to be observed according to our discussion in chapter 3, there do not seem to be any noticeable effects on creditors and taxpayers in this case, nor any instances of "pirate" production. The policy costs in the case of Oregon are unknown, but do not seem to be important in the long run given that the system is administered by the producers and that these costs are taken into account by them.

In the perspective just presented, the outcome of an Oregon-type deposit–refund system seems to be, in terms of benefits, reduced littering and lower waste management costs, and in terms of costs, higher consumer prices for the different beverage and container disposal packages. This essentially requires a political decision on whether or not the benefits outweigh the costs, with the value of reduced littering being the major aspect unknown after the economic analysis. If *energy* is underpriced or energy saving is a merit want, this aspect has to be added to the benefit side (as seems to have been done in some crude fashion in most of the evaluations made of the Oregon case). Moreover, if the evaluation relates to a rapid introduction of the mandatory deposit (as rapid as seems to have been the case in Oregon, where legislation was passed in July 1971 and became effective in October 1972), there are special transition costs that may be important. Thus many of the actual evaluations of the Oregon case observe the effects on *employment and wages* and on *capital costs* due to obsolescence. Because these extra costs are voluntary on the part of the government, owing to a wish to have the system working at an early stage (assuming no chronic long-run unemployment problems), they should hardly be taken to burden the system. Or, they could be esti-

---

[15] Ibid., pp. 108–109.

mated for phasing-in periods of various lengths in a consistent fashion when making comparisons with alternative policy solutions.

If we compare the mandatory deposit–refund system with *a ban on nonrefillable containers* and interpret the latter policy alternative to mean that the market-generated deposit–refund system on refillable bottles is extended to 100 percent of the beverage market, there need not be much of a difference. In particular, if the mandatory minimum deposit is not set at a higher level than the existing market deposit, the only difference would be that the containers not returned would be bottles instead of cans with a consequent change in convenience and in the composition of waste and litter. The convenience effect would be found in the fact that consumers who prefer cans are forced to use bottles. And if, in addition, glass in litter and waste is considered to be worse than metal, the overall effect of the ban would be less attractive than that of the mandatory deposit.[16]

Another alternative would be to introduce a *tax on all beverage containers* produced. Because the tax would be distributed over beverage units depending on trippage rates, the tax would favor returnable containers. At an *ex post* trippage rate of ten and a 5-cent tax on nonreturnables, the tax impact on returnables would be only 0.5 cent. If the market-generated deposit rate did not change, the overall effect would be similar to that of the mandatory deposit with two exceptions. First, beverage prices would be sure to rise more, as beverages in returnable bottles cannot completely avoid the tax. Second, cans—the only nonrefillable alternative likely to remain—cannot be returned, which means that consumers who would like to qualify for a refund but have a preference for (nonbreakable) cans will be discriminated against, in comparison with their treatment under the deposit–refund system of 5 cents on all containers.[17] Hence with deposits the same in the two alternatives, there would be more losers among the consumers (and perhaps also among the producers, especially if the tax were not fully shifted to consumers). Moreover, the tax would lead to only a small reduction in waste management costs and in littering, again because of the nonreturnability of cans.

---

[16] Attempts at estimating the total effects of bans on nonreturnables have been made. See, for example, L. D. Orr, "Profits in Bottle Laws," *Environment*, December 1976.

[17] In fact, in an EPA study of this 5 percent tax case, nonreturnables were assumed to disappear from the market. See U.S. Environmental Protection Agency, *The Beverage Container Problem* (Washington, D.C., U.S. Government Printing Office, 1972).

Thus for the tax to come out as the optimal policy alternative, these negative effects would have to be outweighed by a high government evaluation of the revenue arising in this case.

An alternative often discussed in this context is the *product charge*. Although proposals for introducing this instrument usually refer to the solid waste management problem as a whole and particularly to all kinds of packaging, we here observe only the impact on containers for beer and soft drinks. According to a proposal to the U.S. Congress in 1978, such containers would be charged 0.5 cent per unit. Thus there would be an impact on beverage prices regardless of container type (estimated at 2.2 percent for beer and 4.1 percent for soft drinks). The price effect on beverages in containers actually returned would be about the same as that achieved under the 5-cent tax alternative, assuming that trippage rates would remain around ten. For containers that are not returned, the price effect of the product charge is again about 0.5 cent, whereas in the deposit–refund, ban, and 5-cent-tax alternatives, the price effect would be about 5 cents. In other words, there is no incentive to reduce littering, and so on, by returning containers under the product charge system. The only effect is to reduce total beverage consumption regardless of container type by adding a crude average cost charge of 0.5 cent for littering and waste management.[18] Thus the product charge can hardly be regarded as an alternative to the other instruments discussed here (see chapter 3).

Comments

We have so far studied deposit–refund systems applied only to containers for beer and soft drinks. The reason for this is that most applications and most of the analysis thereof have been limited to these beverages. The potential field of application is of course much larger, involving, to begin with, all kinds of liquids. There are applications of deposit–refund systems to milk in the United Kingdom, Canada, Japan, and Holland, mineral water in the Federal Republic of Germany, and wines and spirits in France, Switzerland, and the Scandinavian countries.[19]

---

[18] Here it should be noted that most econometric studies seem to indicate that beverage consumption is relatively price inelastic (see OECD, *Beverage Containers*, p. 92).

[19] OECD, *Beverage Containers*, pp. 25–29.

It should be stressed that application of deposit–refund systems to the beverage market do not require that containers are refillable. As is indicated by the Oregon type of mandatory deposits, nonrefillable containers also can be included. Here the additional question is whether recycling or some other sort of waste disposal constitutes the superior treatment alternative (that is, the alternative providing the highest V value). It is not always understood that whatever happens to the products returned, there is the positive effect of mandatory deposits on littering and normally, at least, a minimum effect in terms of reduced waste disposal costs.[20] It is a separate issue whether trippage rates tend to be so high and economies of scale such that the refillable container replaces other kinds of containers after the deposit–refund system has been operating for some time.

This leads to a consideration of possible long-term effects of deposit–refund systems for beverage containers. Little in terms of empirical data seems to be available here. The brief recent period of applied deposit–refund systems and the regional limitations of these applications might imply that many of the technological changes and other adaptations to a long-term and a large-scale deposit–refund system have yet to appear. Future change may affect the choice between refillable and recyclable containers or may produce new forms of disposable containers. Thus there may be a long-term rise in the reuse value V. The Canadian refillable plastic milk jug (carrying a 35-cent deposit!) and perhaps also the metal can without detachable parts may be examples here. Such changes could affect market deposit rates—if mandatory systems are designed to allow a sufficient degree of flexibility—and hence influence the littering and return propensities of the consumers.

Over time there may be openings for government-initiated changes in the design of the deposit–refund system. One of these may be an intervention into container standardization for certain or even all beverages. The risk inherent in such schemes is of course the built-in rigidity of standards—especially if they extend across various jurisdictional borders. With built-in rules allowing standards to be revised at regular intervals or with, at least, a deposit differentiation as in Oregon (2 cents on "standard" containers, 5 cents on others), certain safeguards may be provided. But even without any success in the construction of such provisions, it is possible to arrive at a stage here, as in other standardization cases, where the risks appear to be acceptable and where the potential gains of standardiza-

[20] See, for example, OECD, *Beverage Containers,* p. 122.

tion seem substantial. Thus with the kind of attention to the container problem that a flexible deposit–refund system provides, there is the chance that an increased number of policy options will emerge in the long run.

One of the options available right now is that instead of having the deposit surplus stay with the producers, as seems to have been the design chosen in all deposit–refund applications to beverage containers, the deposit surplus can be turned over to the government as we assumed in chapters 3 and 4. One disadvantage of the latter arrangement is that it requires additional administrative costs for checking the amounts to be transferred to the government. But a disadvantage of the former design is, as we have already pointed out, that it may provide certain short-term incentives to producers, especially small producers, to collect the deposit but, at the same time, to take measures to discourage container returns. This is definitely a risk if the full refund payment exceeds the net reuse value V of the returned container; in that case the return of an additional container represents a net loss to the producer. Thus it would appear as if the full refund payment must fall short of V to ensure a smooth performance of the deposit–refund system. This is an important issue particularly because the socially correct payment, as we have shown in chapter 3, should exceed V as long as the propensity to return containers is sensitive to the refund rate. In fact, the deposit should then equal A, the nonmarket benefit (for example, the expected negative external effects avoided), and be added to the reuse value, which is positive in the case of refillable containers. In other words, the consumer should be given $R + V = A + V$ unless a maximum return rate could be achieved at a lower refund rate (see figure 3-4). If the deposit has to be lower than V, we can hardly expect that the deposit–refund system in general will lead to a social optimal position. Thus, if return rates are sensitive to the size of the refund and if there are obstructions from the market when payments to consumers exceed V—such as, by making returns more difficult and hence increasing C_R—the efficient solution could be to let the government collect the deposit surplus.

Finally, it should be noted that if V is maximized when the container is turned over to someone other than the original (type of) producers, a transfer of deposits may in any case be required for the system to be efficient. In other words, a stipulation that requires that deposits remain with the original producers could limit the competition in the reuse and reprocessing market and thus add another potential source of inefficiency.

OTHER APPLICATIONS
OF DEPOSIT–REFUND SYSTEMS

Waste Lubrication Oil

It has been estimated that some 25 percent of the 2 million tons of oil reaching the oceans each year originates from automobile oils.[21] Although data of this type are very uncertain, it seems clear that some of the lubrication oil used in vehicles, by industry, and so on eventually affects surface water quality and has negative effects on marine life and people. Moreover, if improperly discharged to landfills, and elsewhere, waste lubrication oil affects groundwater quality, possibly being a source of carcinogenic hydrocarbons in drinking water. If incinerated without removal of contaminants, it affects air quality. And if discharged into sewage systems, it increases treatment costs. Finally, if oil is underpriced from a social (global) point of view, present recovery rates may be suboptimal, adding a possible conservation problem to the environmental and waste treatment problems of waste lubrication oil.

As can be seen from the illustrations of the "waste oil path" in figure 5-1, some 50 percent of lubrication oil use is in the automobile sector, and some 50 percent or more of all lubrication oil is considered to be recoverable, according to data for the United States in 1972 and the Federal Republic of Germany in 1971. Actual recovery, including re-refining (to lubrication oil), and uses as fuel and as material for road construction amounted to about one third of sales. Because of differences in use patterns, in particular, international comparisons are difficult to make. It may be noted, however, that the two countries cited by Pearce (1975) are among those with the highest official recovery rates among the OECD countries.[22]

The "nonrecoverable" part of lubrication oil sales is determined by present levels of oil combustion, leakages, and so on. The "recoverable" waste oil is not of homogeneous quality; the major part of it has a 10 percent maximum impurity (402 tons for Germany in 1971). Different qualities of waste lubrication oil (WLO) have different optimal forms of reprocessing (for a given institutional setup) or different maximum reuse

---

[21] See *Man's Impact on the Global Environment* (Cambridge, Mass., MIT Press, 1970).

[22] See D. W. Pearce, *Economic Instruments and the Control of Waste Lubrication Oil* (Paris, Organization for Economic Cooperation and Development, 1975).

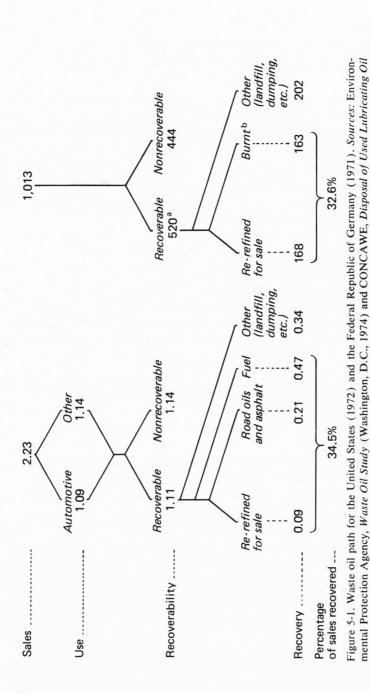

Figure 5-1. Waste oil path for the United States (1972) and the Federal Republic of Germany (1971). *Sources:* Environmental Protection Agency, *Waste Oil Study* (Washington, D.C., 1974) and CONCAWE, *Disposal of Used Lubricating Oil in Western Europe* (The Hague, 1973), both as cited in D. Pearce, *Economic Instruments and the Control of Waste Lubrication Oil* (Paris, Organization for Economic Cooperation and Development, 1975).

[a] Varying definitions explain why 520 falls short of the sum of $168 + 163 + 202 = 531$.
[b] Assumed to be used, or possible to use, as fuel.

values (V). Thus the WLO collected appears in principle as a differentiated product, like different beverage containers, with different optimal postcollection uses.

Countries vary in their policies with respect to the WLO problems, ranging from regulations alone to financial incentives for one or several reuses of the product. In Germany a combination of taxes on fresh lubrication oil and differentiated subsidies on reprocessing and reuse of WLO has been implemented. This policy amounts to a version of a deposit–refund system with the deposit surplus held by the federal government. In the following, this system will be presented and discussed in some detail, based on the study by Pearce.[23]

The principles and results of the German deposit–refund system. Since 1969, fresh lubrication oil has carried an additional tax of 75 DM[24] per ton, which is held in a special federal reserve fund to be used for subsidies of WLO collectors and reprocessors. A subsidy of 120 DM per ton is paid for refining WLO into lubrication oil, 102 DM per ton for certain reprocessing, such as heating oils, and 100–126 DM per ton for incineration depending on the purification process used. Although the variation in subsidy rates is small, it can be viewed as a differentiation based on the reuse values (V) and external effects (A) of each particular form of WLO reprocessing. In principle, this system can be regarded as a 75 DM deposit–refund rate (excluding interest) and a 25–51 DM additional payment depending on $A + V$ variations among end uses. (In actual fact, however, the relative levels of the taxes and subsidies seem to have been determined so as to achieve a balanced "WLO budget.")

Germany is divided into WLO collection regions. Private collection firms are assigned regions in such a way that any one disposer will face at least two competitive collectors. When called upon, collectors are required to collect all individual quantities exceeding 200 liters and to provide disposers with containers for future WLO, if asked for. For impurities higher than 10 percent, collectors may charge the disposer according to a set of federally approved rates. This means that the subsidy rate structure in fact is more differentiated than was suggested above. More-

[23] OECD later made a more detailed and up-to-date study of the waste oils recovery in the Federal Republic of Germany (prepared by Paul Plechatsch, Federal Office for Trade and Industry, Bonn), November 1978, unpublished.

[24] All figures here refer to the system's initial period around 1970. At the time, 1 DM (Deutschmark) was approximately 50 cents (U.S.).

over, it means that disposers have an incentive to call a collector when the disposer's return cost (C_R) does not exceed the alternative disposal cost (C_d), which seems likely for low-impurity WLO but less certain for other qualities.

The results of the system are reported to be that the federal reserve fund was "directly involved in the disposal of over 40 percent of all waste oil, with industry disposing of most of the remainder, only 7 or 8 percent being unaccounted for."[25] The reserve fund showed a financial surplus for 1969–1971.[26]

Comments. This system is designed to create competition in the reprocessing industry (presumably in terms of service quality only, as prices are regulated), to allow the reprocessing market to adjust to relative reuse values and relative external effects and to let differences in these respects for different levels of contamination of WLO be transferred to the disposers and hence to the users of lubrication oil. As the system now operates, there is the risk, however, that disposers of heavily contaminated oil will prefer to dispose of it in ways other than having it picked up by collectors at a charge. Moreover, the present version of the system leaves disposers of small quantities (such as motorists making "do-it-yourself" oil changes) outside the system because of the 200-liter limit for obligatory collection by reprocessing firms.

Adjustments of the rules of the system are possible that could remedy both of these possible shortcomings. Increasing the subsidy refund level to achieve a positive price for the disposer of heavily contaminated oil (and an even higher price for less contaminated oil) would ensure a higher recovery rate for these waste products. And such a change may lead to establishing, say, gas station intermediaries to collect waste oil from small consumers. For financial or distributional policy reasons, the tax (deposit) rate may have to be increased as well.

Again, additional effects are to be expected in the long run from a system of this kind. Such effects would work via incentives on technology development toward reducing lubrication oil demand, reducing the "non-recoverable" part of oil use (by reducing leakages and so on), reducing

[25]Pearce, *Economic Instruments*, p. 25.

[26] The results of the German system are interesting, provided of course, that recovery rates otherwise would have been significantly lower. This is a pertinent provision, in particular because we saw in figure 5-1 that the U.S. recovery rate was at least as high as the German one. The reason for the "high" U.S. rate is unknown.

the contamination of waste oil, inducing standardization of WLO at the collection stage, improving treatment processes and adjusting the'n to large-scale supply, and so on.

The deposit–refund system, or the combined tax-subsidy system, is, of course, not the only policy alternative to bring about many of the short-run and long-run effects now mentioned. But the alternatives—product charges, subsidies alone, regulation with fines—involve the problems pointed out earlier (see in particular the end of chapter 3). The fact that policy costs may be lower for some of these alternatives would of course affect the policy choice. But although the design of the German version of this system is quite ambitious, with record-keeping requirements on both sides of the market and with an attempt to achieve an effective regional organization, the experience does not seem to have revealed any prohibitive costs of this kind. In fact, the system is reported to have been taken as a model for policy in all countries of the European Economic Community.

Junked Cars

In many countries, abandoned automobiles have presented an increasing externality problem. Especially when junk yards do not offer attractive prices for junked cars—because of low scrap prices, high transportation costs, and so on—discarded cars have been left in parking lots, in forests, in rivers, and in lakes. For a number of reasons, such cars cannot be taken care of until considerable time has passed. Meanwhile, they are often turned into "dismembered corpses" by scavenging motorists looking for spare parts, tires, and so on, thus becoming even more conspicuous eyesores.

In Sweden a deposit–refund system was introduced in 1976 to remedy this problem. The same solution has more recently been proposed for other countries, such as Norway (where it was introduced in 1978), and for the state of New Mexico in the United States.[27] A similar system has been in operation in the state of Maryland, although the effects there seem to have been rather limited. In this section, we look at the Swedish system, which so far appears to have had a successful period as well as

---

[27] For the latter case, see F. Lee Brown and A. O. Lebeck, *Cars, Cans and Dumps* (Baltimore, The Johns Hopkins University Press for Resources for the Future, 1976) pp. 110–111.

a less successful one because of certain inadequacies of the system design.[28]

Swedish car owners who turn over their hulks to authorized junk dealers—or, in some cases, to reception points run by the local government—get a bonus of 300 Swedish Crowns (SCrs; about $60) per car. Buyers of new cars pay a fee in the same amount (originally 250 SCrs) to finance these bonus payments. This is obviously a version of a deposit–refund system, with the deposit equal to the refund and with the deposits funded by the government. But the deposits paid on new cars are not funded to be used when these cars are junked in the future, perhaps some 10–15 years later. Instead, the deposits are used right away to finance "refunds" (subsidies) to car owners who junk their cars now without necessarily having paid a deposit. But, as total current deposits exceed current refund payments (by some 50 percent), a surplus has accumulated. Part of this surplus has been used to finance local efforts to clean up the environment and rid it of old car wrecks.

Only those junk dealers who see to it that the hulks are subjected to final processing, by fragmentation or other approved form of conversion into metal scrap, are given the necessary authorization. The authorized dealers may be required to furnish security ensuring that the junk yard will be restored if the activity should cease—another application of deposit–refund systems (see chapter 4). They may also be required to collect wrecks in a certain area. Moreover, they cannot refuse to accept cars that are turned over to them. But they can charge a fee for taking care of the hulks, making the net receipts to the car owner fall short of the bonus payment.

During the first year of this system, a reduction in the number of abandoned vehicles seems to have occurred. Unfortunately, however, no evaluation program had been planned in advance by the authorities. Thus the possibilities for analyzing the effects of the new system on the volume of abandoned vehicles and on the number of cars being scrapped were very limited. The studies made by two Swedish government agencies, the Environment Protection Agency (Naturvårdsverket) and the Traffic Safety Agency (Statens trafiksäkerhetsverk), both of which were

---

[28] The Norwegian and the Swedish deposit–refund systems for car hulks are described in two unpublished reports to OECD in September 1978 ("The Recovery of Car Hulks in Norway" by J. Thompson, Norwegian Ministry of Environment, and "The Recovery of Car Hulks in Sweden" by K. L. Astedt, Swedish Environmental Protection Board, respectively.)

asked to analyze the effects of the system in 1978, had almost no detailed results and clear-cut conclusions.[29] Two observations of interest emerge from these studies, however. One is that car owners during the latter part of 1975 to some extent postponed junking their cars until 1976 when the subsidy had been introduced, thus indicating some degree of response to the economic stimulus. The other is that, initially, the number of privately junked cars seems to have dropped significantly in favor of having the hulks taken care of by the authorized junk dealers. The latter effect was important in that it implied a change from a junking procedure regarded as environmentally unsafe to one that was safe.

This possibly favorable development definitely seems to have changed after some time, however. In 1977 and 1978, hulks are said to have reappeared in the environment at presystem rates. The reasons for this change seem obvious. First, the bonus payments were eroded by the high rate of inflation; thus the real value of the refund fell from 300 SCrs in January 1976 to less than 200 SCrs in the end of 1978. Second, and even more important, the design of the system was such that return incentives were affected by scrap prices and other factors influencing the junk dealer's service charge. As soon as a year or two after the system was initiated, service charges had increased from 0 to 200 SCrs in some areas. The main reason was that the 130 SCrs per ton of car scrap that junk dealers got during the boom in 1975 had turned into a payment of 20 SCrs per ton to have hulks processed by the fragmentation industry two years later; that is, there was a price decline of 150 SCrs.

In other words, the deposit–refund system was so designed that inflation and declining scrap prices made the real net receipts per car drop by as much as 75 percent in two years, that is, from 300 SCrs net to 100 SCrs $(300 - 200)$ in current prices or to 75 SCrs in constant prices. It is hardly astonishing that the return rates are significantly affected by such changes in net receipts, especially since a car that is to be junked in most cases must be transported to the junk yard at a high extra cost $(C_R > C_d)$ for the owner. Thus, *in toto,* the net payment may have dropped to a negative value in certain areas.

In line with the analysis in chapter 3, this could of course represent a socially optimal adjustment in net receipts, that is, $R + V_c = A + V$, and hence in return rates.[30] This would be the case if the refund (R) was

[29] See the mimeographed reports (in Swedish) sent to the government by these agencies of June 20 and August 18, 1978, respectively.

[30] As defined earlier, V_c is the payment to the seller of scrap, net of any refund payment, whereas V is the value for the buyer.

determined so as to correspond to the value of the externality or extra waste collection costs avoided (A) and if market prices for scrap, net of service charges, were transferred to car owners without excessive profits among junk dealers or reprocessors; that is, if $V_c = V$. But, except perhaps for densely populated areas, where competition among scrap buyers will keep V_c at a maximum, V_c is likely to be less than V. Under such conditions, it would be necessary to make an adjustment of R to have return incentives on an optimal level. In fact, optimal R should probably have been even higher, as the processing installations for large-scale scrapping of cars have created low-cost recycling facilities for other kinds of fragmentable scrap such as household appliances (refrigerators, freezers, stoves, washing machines, dish washers, and so on).[31]

More important, however, is to question whether in fact there has been a situation in which R is approximately equal to A, as determined by a purely political decision. In any case, it can hardly be regarded as rational to have the degree of approximation of this equality determined by inflation; it would make more sense to have an index system by which the estimated A value in the base year was kept intact in real terms, thus keeping incentives unchanged in this respect. Another possible interpretation, however, is that the base year refund of 300 SCrs represented a value that was originally believed to be sufficient for some maximum return rate at $V_c > 0$. If so, the reductions in V_c (down to -200 SCrs) that occurred later should have been balanced by increases in R in order to keep $R + V_c$ constant.

In conclusion, there is reason to expect that a deposit–refund system for junked cars would work, provided that a minimum flexibility is built into the system. Thus nominal refund (and deposit) rates would have to keep pace with inflation by continuous or frequent adjustments. And unless the refund is high enough to cover the estimated social damage of car wrecks discarded in the environment, refund rates must be tied to, and vary inversely with, the net scrap value as derived from quotations on the scrap market. Both these considerations could be formalized by index clauses guiding the refund rate.

Moreover, we might expect that overall efficiency of the system would be enhanced by creating conditions favorable to competition among (authorized) junk dealers—in line with the German waste lubrication oil system, for example—and by taking into account the interdependency between high volumes of car scrapping and costs for processing of con-

---

[31] See Jarl Höglund, *End Processing of Car Wrecks* (Halmstad, Sweden, Bilfragmentering AB, 1976) (mimeo).

sumer durables, and so on. Both of these aspects would tend to raise the optimal net scrap value (V_c) paid to car owners.

Charter Flight Packages

In the waste lubrication oil case we dealt with a deposit–refund system in which the deposits were paid by producers. We now discuss another application of producer-paid systems, but one that does not require deposit payments in cash. This is also an application to the field of consumer policy.

The rapid growth of foreign travel after the Second World War has partly been made possible by charter flights (and charter bus trips) at prices below regular fares and by convenient comprehensive travel arrangements. Thus traveling abroad is no longer reserved for daring adventurers or high-income groups with proficiency in foreign languages and knowledge of foreign institutions. This became true in particular for the Scandinavian countries. The growing tourist business there led to the appearance of a large number of travel agencies and charter transportation firms. A general tendency to overexpansion, as well as the fact that tourism is sensitive to business cycles, led to a number of business failures, in particular among newly established travel agencies with insufficient financial resources and poor knowledge of the trade. As a consequence, a number of tourists never took the trips they had paid for or were stranded in foreign places with neither the room and board nor the return ticket they had paid for. In some cases the government helped them to get back; in other cases, charter tourists had to pay expensive regular fares to get back on their own.

As it turned out, it was difficult for consumers to know which firms they could rely on, especially since some firms established in the market long ago also went bankrupt. Moreover, low prices alone seem to have been an irresistible temptation for many potential travelers. Therefore the Swedish government intervened in the market in 1967. A law was passed making it necessary for firms selling travel packages to post a bond guaranteeing payment by a bank or an insurance company. A government agency was to determine the amount of the bond on the basis of the form and the size of the firm's operations. If the travel arrangements were canceled, the bond could be used to repay prepayments made by consumers. If the arrangement was interrupted, the bond could be used to finance the completion of the package tour, to bring the tourists home, and to compensate them for the inconvenience caused by the interruption. The extent of these payments is determined by a council with representatives for consumers and the travel industry.

This system cannot be said to have eliminated all the problems for customers of failing travel firms.[32] But it has provided a substantial minimum guarantee to those affected. In addition, it seems to have led to a significant reduction in the number of bankruptcies and incomplete travel arrangements. Moreover, the average annual amount of total payments from the bonds was 285,000 SCrs in 1967–1972 and 186,000 SCrs in 1972–1976, more or less gradually decreasing toward 0 in 1977 (in current prices with a 5–10 percent inflation rate). As can be seen from figure 5-2, payments in all cases of bankruptcy (sixteen cases) fell short of the amount of the bond. Payments averaged about 40 percent of the bonds for the firms involved.

The amount of bonds for the industry as a whole grew from 35 million SCrs in March 1968, to 40–48 million in 1971 and 110–158 million in 1977. Thus the ratio of yearly payments out of the total amount of bonds for all firms has been steadily decreasing. With payments equal to the yearly average for 1972–1976 (186,000 SCrs), they represented only some 0.1 percent of the total amount of bonds in 1977. This supports the view commonly held at the time the law was passed that the main purpose of the law probably would be fulfilled simply by the requirement to post a bond and that actual compensatory payments would play a secondary role from a consumer protection point of view.

This remark as well as the construction of the system itself raises the question of what the effects have been on the market structure in the travel industry. It could be argued that the bond requirement (a minimum of 50,000 SCrs from domestic travel firms) would discriminate against small firms and against new entries, thus reducing competition. Although the system is likely to have raised the barrier for small firms entering and remaining in business (and the law may in fact be said to be designed to achieve this), there has not been any evidence of increased concentration in the industry and of any strong element of protection of well-established large companies. In fact, the number of firms in the industry has increased from 57 in 1972 (when the law was slightly revised) to 130 in 1978; that is, it has more than doubled in six years.

---

[32] The following account is based on reports from the Swedish Ministry of Trade, "On Package Tour Guarantees" (in Swedish), *Kommittee-direktiv 1977:116,* and personal correspondence with K. A. Larsson, Resegarantinaemnden, Stockholm, in April 1978.

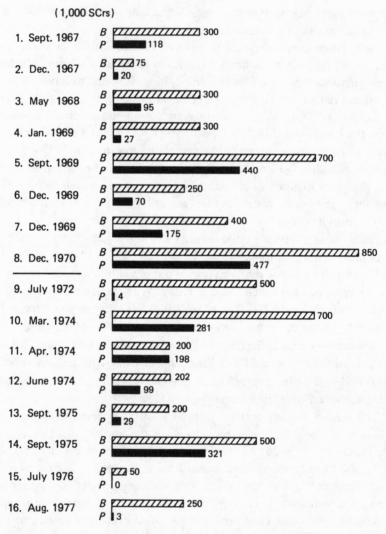

(1,000 SCrs)

1. Sept. 1967	B	300
	P	118
2. Dec. 1967	B	75
	P	20
3. May 1968	B	300
	P	95
4. Jan. 1969	B	300
	P	27
5. Sept. 1969	B	700
	P	440
6. Dec. 1969	B	250
	P	70
7. Dec. 1969	B	400
	P	175
8. Dec. 1970	B	850
	P	477
9. July 1972	B	500
	P	4
10. Mar. 1974	B	700
	P	281
11. Apr. 1974	B	200
	P	198
12. June 1974	B	202
	P	99
13. Sept. 1975	B	200
	P	29
14. Sept. 1975	B	500
	P	321
15. July 1976	B	50
	P	0
16. Aug. 1977	B	250
	P	3

Total bonds in all 16 cases: 5,775   Total Payments: 2,357 (41%)

Figure 5-2. Travel firm bankruptcies in Sweden, total bonds *B* and payments *P* from these bonds, July 1967 to August 1977. *Source:* Swedish Ministry of Trade, "On Package Tour Guarantees" (in Swedish), *Kommittee-direktiv* (1977), p. 116.

The system has had one definite structural effect on the industry. The role of customer advance payments has declined as a source of funds to the companies. The reason is that one of the major factors influencing the prescribed bond amounts was the extent of such advance payments. Thus the system has led to an increased reliance on capital from the firm's own funds, from airline companies, and from external sources on the traditional credit market. At the same time, the bond in itself has reduced the borrowing capacity of the firms for traditional capital needs. These changes have led the industry to demand that it should be allowed to use the capital tied up by the bonds, especially since the total amount of bonds has far exceeded the amount of payments in cases of bankruptcy.

The overprotection that may be said to be inherent in the present version of the bond system has led to larger additions to costs and hence to higher consumer prices than strictly necessary for the industry as a whole. A significant reduction in the size of bonds and the costs therefrom may, however, be difficult to achieve in combination with a requirement specifying a sufficient, separate, financial responsibility for each individual firm. Moreover, it should be pointed out that the role of these costs in total travel cost has been fairly modest. The total cost in terms of interest or premium payments for the 150 million SCrs bond volume in 1977 can be estimated to be at most 5 million SCrs (about 1 percent for banks and up to 4 percent for insurance companies), which represents 0.5 percent of the total volume of sales by the industry in 1977 (1 billion SCrs). However, the Swedish Travel Agency Association estimates that total—direct and indirect—costs are substantially higher, perhaps 25 million SCrs. Thus, given a volume of one million trips in 1977, the cost per trip would be at most 5 SCrs in direct interest or premium payments and at most 25 SCrs ($5), *in toto,* according to the estimate by the association.

To evaluate the consumer's willingness to pay for the effects of the Swedish deposit–refund system for package tours in order to make a comparison with the price increase is not easy. However, during the period when the system has been in operation, consumers have also been given the option to pay an insurance premium of 15–30 SCrs per person for a full refund in case of consumer cancellation due to illness or other unforeseen events. This voluntary price increase of some 1–5 percent of the package tour price, protecting against external risks just as the bond requirement does, has been accepted by 85–90 percent of the consumers. It should be noted, though, that the cancellation risks probably are held to be higher than the bankruptcy risks. But if the attitudes toward these two kinds of risks were considered to be approximately the same, it may be argued that a majority of consumers has had a willingness to pay that exceeds the consumer costs of the bond system and that a minority has been losing a maximum of some 5–25 SCrs, or some 0.5–4 percent of the price of the package tour.

CONCLUDING COMMENTS

We began this chapter by warning the reader that only limited information can be extracted from available empirical studies of applied deposit–refund systems. This is true not only for the more or less superficial observations of applications to waste lubrication oil, junked cars, and service guarantees in the package tour business, but also for the carefully analyzed case of beverage container systems, which revealed several unexplored relationships and conflicting estimates. Against this background we voiced a strong need for future experiments with deposit–refund systems or at least a built-in evaluation phase in full-scale applications of such systems to get more precise information about their effects.

Having sounded this warning, we looked at some of the actual applications of government-initiated deposit–refund systems, trying to cover as much of the ground in the theoretical chapters as possible. We discussed the evidence available from two consumer-paid systems—one with and one without a significant time difference between deposits and refunds (beverage containers and cars, respectively). We also looked at two cases of producer-paid systems—one with and one without cash deposits (waste lubrication oil and package tours, respectively). This last case concerned an issue of consumer policy, whereas the other three dealt with issues of environmental and conservation policy.

In the final chapter we turn to a detailed presentation of two further possible applications of deposit–refund systems. One is related to the environmental problem caused by the use of cooling equipment (with effects on the ozone layer), where consumer- and producer-paid cash deposits and short-term as well as long-term refund prospects could provide an effective policy device. In the other case, producer-paid cash or credit deposits could help to reduce a consumer and a conservation problem by creating a guarantee of a time-limited supply of spare parts for consumer durables. In both cases—in particular, in the latter—the objective is to present an illustrative sketch of a possible application rather than a ready-made proposal for a new deposit–refund system.

6 TWO POTENTIAL APPLICATIONS

INTRODUCTION

Refrigerant use of chlorofluoromethanes (CFM) is second to aerosol use as a source of ozone depletion by CFM emissions, that is, depletion of the global ozone layer in the stratosphere. So far, political action has been taken only with respect to aerosol use of CFM—by introducing a ban on so-called nonessential applications (for example, in the United States, Norway, and Sweden). For various reasons, optimal control of the refrigerant use of CFM may require policy instruments other than bans or similar regulatory measures. A possible policy alternative is a deposit–refund system on cooling equipment with a deposit (tax) on CFM used and a refund (subsidy) on CFM recovered, that is, CFM not released into the atmosphere. The economic implications of using such a system are discussed in the first part of this chapter.[1]

In the second part we discuss the general features of a system that would provide guaranteed availability of spare parts for certain consumer products. We start by presenting the case for when spare part availability

[1] For an approximate outline of a concrete deposit–refund system applied to cooling equipment in the United States, the reader is referred to Peter Bohm, "Protecting the Ozone Layer: The Case of Controlling Refrigerant Uses of CFMs," chapter 12 in John H. Cumberland, James R. Hibbs, and Irving Hoch, eds. "The Economics of Managing Chlorofluorocarbons: Stratospheric Ozone and Climate Issues" (Washington, D.C., Resources for the Future, 1981).

is to be considered a market-failure problem and how a government-initiated deposit–refund system could be an appropriate solution to this problem. The possible effects on the markets involved are discussed in general terms.

PROTECTING THE OZONE LAYER: THE CASE OF CONTROLLING REFRIGERANT USES OF CHLOROFLUOROMETHANES

There is some evidence—incomplete but hardly refutable—of a potentially serious ozone problem. In particular, certain chemicals used for aerosol sprays, refrigeration, and so on, as well as nitrogen fertilizers, will eventually be released into the atmosphere and through turbulence reach the ozone shield located in the lower part of the stratosphere after some time. The resulting reduction of the ozone shield will increase the radiation of ultraviolet light and thus have detrimental effects on human health (primary skin cancer), animal life, plants, and certain materials.

If the relative contribution of different economic activities to the depletion of the ozone shield were known, an efficient distribution of ozone protection could be achieved by equalizing the net marginal social cost for reductions of all the activities involved—release of CFMs,[2] use of nitrogen fertilizers, and the space shuttle. As the relative contribution in fact is not known, there will have to be separate decisions for each activity. The use of CFM is an activity of particular interest because there seem to be good prospects, relatively speaking, for a global willingness to control this activity. Since nonessential uses of aerosol are banned in the United States and a few other countries and given that this ban will spread and sharply reduce the use of CFM as a propellant, the remaining major use will be that of CFM as a refrigerant (see table 6-1).

The refrigerant use of CFM presents two severe policy problems. First, there do not seem to be any compounds that are easily substitutable for those CFMs currently used as refrigerants; existing substitutes are expensive, flammable, toxic, or corrosive. Thus there can be no simple adjustment of technology with commensurate small effects on consumers and producers as was possible in the aerosol case. Second, the durability of

[2] Only CFMs labelled F-11 and F-12 are taken to be detrimental to the ozone layer.

Table 6-1. Distribution of 1974 End Uses of F-11 and F-12

End uses	United States	Total OECD
Aerosol	61.8	65.9
Refrigerant	23.3	18.1
Plastics	8.7	12.1
Other	6.2	3.9
Total	100.0	100.0

Source: Organization for Economic Cooperation and Development, Environment directorate (Paris, unpublished material, 1977).

existing cooling equipment means that the current stock of such equipment will remain an important source of CFM emissions for a long period to come. This means that we are actually confronted with two policy objectives—reducing CFM releases from existing equipment and reducing releases from new equipment—which also differs from the aerosol case, where product durability and releases from existing sprays were not a matter of major concern.

Table 6-2 lists available estimates of CFM emissions in 1973 by major forms of cooling equipment. (E denotes emissions with a first subscript indicating stage of use: M, manufacture; U, normal use; S, repair and service operations; and D, disposal. A second subscript distinguishes between new (N) and existing (E) equipment. For example, E_{SE} denotes emissions from servicing of existing equipment.) Although the source of those data[3] notes questions on their reliability, they are useful in indicating probable orders of magnitude. Thus disposal emissions account for some 23 percent of total CFM releases, whereas the rest can be attributed to emissions from use, repair, and servicing operations.

A reduction of future CFM emissions can occur at any of the emission stages identified in our classification. Table 6-3 lists the ways in which such reductions can be made, in addition, of course, to limiting CFM emissions by reducing the use of cooling equipment.

Table 6-4 lists selected policy instruments that could be used to bring about the changes given in table 6-3. Ideally, we would like to estimate the social costs of using these instruments in order to establish a social marginal cost (SMC) function for reducing CFM emissions and compare that

[3] G. C. Eads and coauthors, *Non-Aerosol Chlorofluorocarbon Emissions: Evaluation of EPA Supplied Data* (Santa Monica, Calif., Rand, December 1977).

Table 6-2. Releases in Million Pounds of CFM (Primarily F-11 and F-12) from Cooling Equipment in the United States in 1978

Equipment	$E_{UE} + E_{SE}$[a]		E_{DE}[a]	Total
Automotive air conditioners (some F-22)[b]	49.6	(42.8)[c]	21.3	70.9
Home refrigerators, freezers, ice makers, and dehumidifiers	1.7[d]		3.3[d]	5.0[d]
Commercial cooling equipment (some F-22 and F-502)[b]	28.4	(20.4)[c]	5.4	33.8
Chillers (some F-22 and F-502)[b,e]	31.1	(23.4)[c]	2.8	33.9
Total	110.8		32.8	143.6

Source: G. C. Eads and coauthors, *Non-Aerosol Chlorofluorocarbon Emissions: Evaluation of EPA Supplied Data* (Santa Monica, Calif., Rand, December 1977) p. VI. 5.

 [a] For definitions, see text.

 [b] CFMs F-22 and F-502 are not taken to be detrimental to the ozone layer.

 [c] Values in parentheses are the maximum recoverable at the repair and service stages. These values are reported by A. D. Little (see Eads and coauthors, *Non-Aerosol Chlorofluorocarbon Emissions*) as potentially recoverable through relatively minor modifications to current equipment design or service procedures.

 [d] Probably too low. $E_{UE} + E_{SE}$ may be as high as 3 million lb according to the Du Pont Company ("Information Requested by EPA on Non-Aerosol Propellant Uses" mimeo. [Wilmington, Del., March 15, 1978] p. III-29), and E_{DE} for 1976 is 4.5 according to another estimate reported, Eads and coauthors, *Non-Aerosol Chlorofluorocarbon Emissions*, p. B-26.

 [e] Chillers are large air-conditioning units for commercial uses (see Eads and coauthors, *Non-Aerosol Chlorofluorocarbon Emissions*, appendix D).

with a social marginal benefit (SMB) function for the resulting reductions in ozone depletion (see figure 6-1). Given the vast uncertainty as to the effects of CFM emissions on the ozone layer and the impact of variations in the ozone layer, the latter function cannot be established at the present time. Thus the choice of optimal policy, that is, optimal reduction in CFM emissions, will have to be determined by a political decision of how much social cost is acceptable for additional reductions of emissions. In other words, given a SMC curve ranking policy instruments in the order of increasing social marginal costs for reductions in CFM emissions, a cutoff point would have to be determined by the government's willingness to make known sacrifices for unknown benefits.

Owing to the lack of data at the present time, we cannot even determine the social costs of the different policy instruments. Thus the SMC curve will essentially be an abstraction until extensive analyses have been carried out. However, on the basis of a set of innocent-looking assumptions we could make some progress in evaluating the policy options in this area.

Table 6-3. Possible Measures Reducing CFM Release by Source

		E_M:	Change of production technology Reduce CFM per unit Substitute other refrigerant
E_{UE}:	Speed up service Replace old units	E_{UN}:	Design changes Speed up service (Replace old units)
E_{SE}:	Service procedure changes Scrap instead of service/repair	E_{SN}:	Design changes Service procedure changes Scrap instead of service/repair
E_{DE}:	Recovery of CFM Destruction of CFM	E_{DN}:	Recovery of CFM Destruction of CFM

Table 6-4. Selected Instruments to Enforce Measures Reducing CFM Release

	Regulation	Economic incentives
E_M:	Ban on high-CFM-releasing production technology Ban on high CFM contents per unit Ban on CFM as a refrigerant	Tax on CFM use or subsidies on CFM savings
E_U:	Standards on design of new equipment to reduce leakage under normal use Inspection of units at regular intervals and service if required (or disposal)	Tax on recharge
E_S:	Standards on design for easy service without CFM release Standards for service and repair work	Tax on recharge Subsidy on refrigerants collected
E_D:	Ban on improper storage or disposal of CFM-containing equipment	Subsidy on proper disposal of CFM-containing equipment

First, we may note that in general both regulation and economic incentives may be used for each instance of emission reduction (E_M and so on), given that they do not have exactly the same function. Thus a ban or a standard may guarantee a certain minimum reduction in emissions but provide little or no incentive to cut down on emissions below this minimum level. Economic incentive schemes may play the latter role with, in particular, effects on long-term behavior in the industry.

Second, economic incentives probably would not be very effective in reducing E_U and E_S. Given that the cost of recharging and servicing cooling equipment consists mainly of labor costs, a tax on the refrigerant

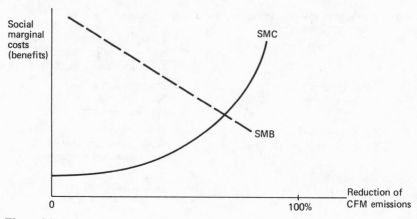

Figure 6-1.

(with a present sale price on the order of $1 to $3 per pound)[4] would have to be very high to speed up service or replacement and stimulate more careful refrigerant-saving servicing operations. To take an example, servicing a home appliance and adding a pound of refrigerant with a tax of 100 percent of the present price would add only a couple of dollars to a service charge of at least $20. A tax on CFM of the order of 100 percent of the present consumer price (which we have used elsewhere as a possible tax level) would probably not have much influence on the willingness to call for a service operation. If so, reductions of E_U and E_S (if at all desired) would probably have to be managed primarily by regulatory instruments.

Third, regulation and economic incentives may change roles when we consider disposal emissions. Here, we know from other fields that existing laws on littering or improper dumping have limited effects, probably because of difficulties of supervision and control. Thus, introducing economic incentives for proper disposal would be required if an effective instrument to reduce E_D is desired.

To sum up the arguments made so far, if optimal policy would involve measures taken at all or most stages of emissions, policy instruments providing economic incentives could be used at least as a supplement to regulatory means, with the exception of the E_D stage, where only incentive instruments would seem to be effective.

[4] Ibid., pp. A-11 and C-15.

Fourth, as we discuss further below, disposal of cooling equipment constitutes a problem even if ozone-depleting effects are not taken into consideration. Old refrigerators, air conditioners, and so on are often dumped or stored where they create hazards to children and damages to aesthetic values.[5] Moreover, if dumped into the municipal waste stream, they add significantly to waste treatment costs. If disposed of in other ways, they have a certain reuse or scrap value. This value might increase in the long run because of design changes, once used units begin to be recovered on a large scale. Even if these factors currently are not in themselves important enough to call for an incentive system for proper disposal (many such proposals exist, however), they might significantly reduce the net social costs of managing the disposal of cooling equipment with regard to the effects of ozone depletion.

Finally, if the disposal problem is taken care of by a subsidy related to the CFM contents and this subsidy is coupled with a tax on the use of CFM, thereby stimulating design changes and reducing the use of CFM, the result will be a policy package of taxes and subsidies or a deposit–refund system that avoids or at least moderates effects on the government budget. The possibility of no or small financial effects of such a package makes it differ from other economic incentive systems in a way that may be quite important from the viewpoint of political acceptability, as we have pointed out earlier. Moreover, given the tax on CFM (affecting E_M) and the subsidy on CFM collected (affecting E_D), there will be economic incentives affecting also E_U and E_S, which may be worthwhile as a part of a larger policy program, although the direct contribution to reducing the CFM emission at these latter stages may be small.

We may sum up as follows. An analysis of the social costs of regulatory measures to control refrigerant CFM emissions will have to be made in order to design an optimal policy with respect to CFM (F-11 and F-12). Given the results of that analysis—but possibly before such results are available—economic incentive schemes may be found to play a role as policy instruments at least as a supplement to regulatory means concerning E_M, E_U, and E_S and as the only effective policy solution with respect to E_D (if optimal policy involves measures on all points of emissions). The social costs of managing E_D may in fact turn out to be rather small,

---

[5] ". . . perhaps the major problem associated with [durable products such as refrigerators] is that they are so often littered or abandoned in alleys or along sideroads." Resources Conservation Committee, *Staff Background Paper No. 4* (Washington, D.C., October 28, 1977) p. 7.

that is, small enough to be incorporated in a policy that considers the total ozone problem. The financing subsidies of reductions of E_D by a tax on CFM use (with its additional beneficial effects on equipment design) will result in a comprehensive incentive system where the use of CFM is made more expensive everywhere (in new and old equipment) and where the collection—and thus the avoided emissions—of CFM will be made less expensive everywhere (in the context of servicing as well as disposal). This system could be seen as an operational approach to eliminating the "non-essential" emissions of CFM used as a refrigerant, without the financial problems of a pure subsidy scheme and without the political disadvantages of a tax scheme introducing a new, inescapable tax (such as a product charge).

First, we present some alternative versions of this system. Second, we investigate the probable overall effects on the economy from the introduction of a deposit–refund system.

Alternative Versions of an Incentive System

If used CFM is to be retrieved instead of being released into the atmosphere, questions arise as to what should be done with it, who should collect it, how should the refunds on collected units be determined, and how should they be financed? After having dealt with these questions, we need to observe alternative ways of determining the deposit (tax) on CFM. Finally, we must consider the particular problems caused by emissions from existing (nondeposit) equipment.

Destruction or reprocessing. It is technically possible both to destroy CFM collected from used equipment without leakage into the atmosphere and to refine collected CFM for reuse.[6] Once the net costs of these two alternatives have been determined, the government may select the least expensive alternative and require its implementation. Because the two alternatives may be cost-ranked in different order for different types of CFMs, for different locations of the collected CFM, and so on, the requirement may be structured on the basis of such factors. However, administrative advantages (such as simplified control procedures) may outweigh such considerations and call for a uniform type of disposal.

---

[6] Du Pont Company, "Information Requested by EPA on Non-Aerosol Propellant Uses," mimeo. (Wilmington, Del., March 15, 1978) pp. III-46–III-49.

Over time, there may be changes in the costs of the different disposal alternatives, and new ones may appear. This is likely to occur not only as a result of normal technical change, but also as a result of changes in the industry induced by the policy measures that are taken. A government might respond to such changes by adjusting its rules on how final disposal should be made. However, the uncertainty of this response (given pressure from industry and unions) is likely to reduce the industry's incentives to develop new alternatives and improve existing ones not currently in use. Instead of determining the disposal of CFM, the government could determine certain required properties of disposal, in terms of units of atmospheric CFM releases, and let the market establish the reprocessing industry that minimizes costs of CFM disposal. This would allow for permanent competition among reprocessing alternatives to minimize costs of reduced CFM emissions. In particular, it would lead to optimal switching among alternatives over time in accordance with cost changes due to technological change. Moreover, if the structure of the reprocessing industry were allowed to be determined by the market, there would be incentives to invest in research and development of new reprocessing solutions and to redesign cooling equipment on the basis of expected reductions in disposal costs.

Regardless of whether the collected CFM is destroyed, reused, or reprocessed in any other sense, the industry may reprocess the discarded *equipment* that contained the CFM. Although induced technical change may produce easily detachable CFM containers or coils, so that these parts of the equipment would become the only ones the reprocessing industry handles, the rest of the equipment may be worth reprocessing, too. This already seems to be the case for certain types of equipment. But it would happen more often if scrapping or reuse of the remaining parts carried a (higher) positive market value once the CFM part were to be collected. Moreover, it should be taken into account that collecting the remaining parts of the equipment could imply the elimination of certain negative external effects, just as the reclamation of the CFM parts is assumed to do. If so, the government would have to be relied upon to transform these reductions of social costs into price signals. Since certain types of cooling equipment are now dumped where they cause externalities and since the equipment is expensive to treat when it appears in the municipal waste stream, a subsidy or refund equal to these social cost savings could make the reduction of CFM releases less costly in the context of an overall recovery program for used cooling equipment.

In summary, the alternatives are that CFM can be reused or destroyed in a reprocessing stage and that the cooling equipment as a whole or the CFM only can be reprocessed. Given economic incentives set equal to the amount of the negative externalities avoided and given the rules for reducing or eliminating CFM emissions by reprocessing, the choice of optimal reprocessing can be left to the market.

Transfer from users to reprocessors. At each point in time there is a given market value V_j of the CFM from equipment type j that has been returned for reprocessing. In some instances, V_j could be positive, although we would expect V_j in the normal case to be negative. The transfer of CFM to the reprocessors can be done in several ways. The user may deliver it himself at an etimated cost of $T_j{}^U$ and "collect" V_j as well as the refund. Or it may be collected by the reprocessor at $V_j - T_j{}^r$, where $T_j{}^r$ is the pickup cost. Or it may be picked up and transferred to the reprocessor by a third party, such as the seller of new cooling equipment, at a price $T_j{}^S$. Given that the user is provided with adequate information about the various alternatives (perhaps from the yellow pages in the local phone book or from a local government information service), he may choose the alternative that minimizes his return cost $C_R{}^i$; that is,

$$C_{Rj}{}^i = \min(T_j{}^U, T_j{}^r, T_j{}^S) \qquad \text{for user } i$$

Thus the collection or transfer activity may be left to the market. There is a caveat, however. If there are economies of scale in this activity, the market may not identify the least-cost alternative, or the alternative established may use some form of monopolistic pricing, or both. In such cases, an alternative might be that the local government give concessions to a collection firm at regulated prices (T_j) for limited periods, ensuring *ex ante* competition among potential holders of the concessions.

Refund payments. We have assumed that the reprocessor and the collector are paid for their services by V_j and T_j, which are market-determined or regulated as is indicated above. Because users would be allowed to return the used products to the reprocessor directly or via a third party and because the reprocessing industry can be expected to be more concentrated than the collectors, it would be practical (for control purposes) for the refund payments to be introduced at the reprocessing stage. Thus, for each unit received by a reprocessing firm, the firm would pay a refund

R_j (for the CFM) directly or indirectly to the user. This means that the user would receive a total amount of $R_j + V_j - C_{Rj}{}^i$ when he returns a used piece of equipment (or the relevant part of it). To avoid fraud when there are several reprocessors who could sell units among each other for additional refunds, each unit of equipment would have to be identifiable, say, by a registration number introduced by the producer (importer of new cooling equipment) or the agency that administers the refund payments, the latter being relevant especially for initially existing equipment. As an alternative, the agency could be made formally responsible for supervising the inflow of all equipment or CFM at the reprocessing plants.

As these remarks suggest, the government would directly finance the refund payments. In other words, the government would try to find a system that prevents fraud and pays refunds to the reprocessing industry for units received. However, as we have indicated earlier, the payment could be organized in a different fashion. If it turns out that the most efficient reprocessing activity is conducted by the original producer of the CFM or of the cooling equipment and if the producer has to introduce a deposit (tax) on new CFM (equipment) sold, he could use the deposits to finance the refunds and deliver only the surplus to the government (or cover the deficit of refunds over deposits from government sources). Or, as an extreme case of this kind, the government may abstain from requiring that a certain deposit be paid on new equipment. Thus, as we saw is true for government intervention in the beverage container industry, when a minimum refund is determined by government, the deposit is simply part of the price for the beverage and thus accrues to the producer to be used for refund payments on containers returned to the producer.

As we have discussed earlier (concerning beverage containers, for example), the latter system has a disadvantage in that the refund rate can hardly be sustained at a level above what the return is worth to the producer.[7] Hence a government subsidy (refund) will be needed when the socially efficient volume of product returns calls for a refund rate above this value. More important, perhaps, is that the turnover in the refrigeration industry is not as rapid as that in the beverage industry. With durability of cooling equipment of the order of ten to twenty years, the deposit and the refund payments would have to be separated even when the producer happens to be the optimal reprocessor. Therefore we

---

[7] By refund we mean here the total payment for product returns, $R + V_j$ in the notation used earlier.

expect the optimal version of a deposit–refund system to be that in which refunds are paid from government to reprocessor.

Optimal refund rate. Assume to begin with that at each point in time there is a given number of units of cooling equipment being discarded ($\bar{X}_{Rj}^{max}$). Without the return alternative, users will dispose of these units in other ways (storing, selling for scrap, dumping in the municipal waste stream, illegal dumping by the user or others, and so on). The cost of the disposal alternative then chosen is $C_{dj}{}^i$ for user i. If the return alternative at costs $C_{Rj}{}^i - V_j$ is introduced, these costs may fall short of $C_{dj}{}^i$. If this is true for all users and the difference $C_{Rj}{}^i - C_{dj}{}^i = \Delta C_j$ is the same for all, users would appear to benefit from the introduction of the new alternative even without any refund. Thus, if $\Delta C_j < V_j$—and in particular if this remains or becomes true in the future after changes of product design or relative prices, or both, have taken place—the market could take care of the CFM disposal problem on its own. But if $\Delta C_j > V_j$, a refund is required for the return alternative to be chosen and sustained by the market. Provided that the marginal social willingness to pay for reducing CFM emissions per unit of equipment j, $SWTP_j$ is at least $\Delta C_j - V_j + \epsilon$, where ϵ is the minimal amount necessary for users to perceive an advantage of the return alternative over the dumping alternative, a refund in this amount will be called for.[8] In practice, V_j is likely to be subject to cyclical variations as well as structural changes, all of which will require adjustments in R_j over time. Given that V_j is market-determined, R_j may be formally tied to V_j, so that changes in V_j immediately result in changes in R_j ($< SWTP_j$) to insure that $R_j = \Delta C_j - V_j + \epsilon$. Changes in ΔC_j may be more complex and thus may have to be countered on an *ad hoc* basis. One reason is that changes here may result in heterogeneous differences, $C_{Rj}{}^i - C_{dj}{}^i$.

In general, we may expect $C_{Rj}{}^i - C_{dj}{}^i$ to differ among users because of differences in locations, transportation facilities, storage facilities, replacement decisions, and so on. Ranking units to be discarded in the order of increasing $C_{Rj}{}^i - C_{dj}{}^i$, we may derive a disposal cost difference curve such as that labeled $\Delta C_j{}^i$ in figure 6-2. If maximum $C_{Rj}{}^i - C_{dj}{}^i = \Delta C_j{}^i$ is below $SWTP_{ij} + V_j - \epsilon$, all discarded units should be returned. If not, the optimal level of units returned will be equal to $X_{Rj}{}^0$ in figure 6-2, which is achieved at a refund $R_j = SWTP_{ij}$.

[8] Here ε is assumed to be the same for all users. $SWTP_j$ is derived from the $SWTP$ per pound of CFM not released into the atmosphere.

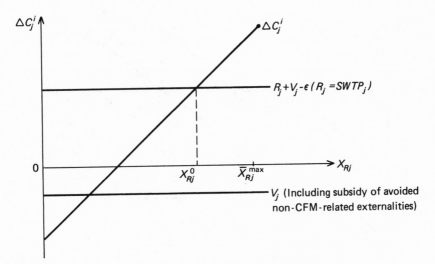

Figure 6-2.

So far we have not taken into account that the introduction of the return alternative and a refund may affect the volume of units taken out of service. As is discussed in more detail in chapter 2, these changes will tend to speed up the termination of use of existing equipment with or without replacement by new equipment. This effect can be expected to be stronger the smaller the $\Delta C_j{}^i$. Thus the introduction of the return alternative alone (that is, $R_j = 0$) will increase disposal at each level of $\Delta C_j{}^i < V_j$, for example, as shown by ab in figure 6-3. Accumulating these increases from minimum $\Delta C_j{}^i$ to $\Delta C_j{}^i = V_j$ will give a total increase equal to ac at $R_j = 0$. Raising R_j from 0 to $SWTP_j$ will add further to these incentives, giving an accumulated propensity to return as shown by PR_j in figure 6-3. For $C_j{}^i > R_j + V_j - \epsilon$, the return alternative will not be used, and thus disposal decisions will not be affected here, leaving unchanged the volume of discarded units not returned. In other words, $\bar{\bar{X}}_{Rj}{}^{\max} - X_{Rj}{}^{\mathrm{opt}}$ in figure 6-3 equals $\bar{X}_{Rj}{}^{\max} - X_{Rj}{}^0$ in figure 6-2, where $\bar{\bar{X}}_{Rj}{}^{max}$ is the total disposal of cooling equipment j.

To conclude, the refund rate R_j will equal the maximum social willingness to pay ($SWTP_j$) unless all discarded units are returned at a lower level of R_j, in which case optimal R_j will equal the minimum value required for a 100 percent return rate. This means that refunds per unit of CFM will be equal for different types of equipment to the extent that maximum $\Delta C_j{}^i$ exceeds $SWTP_j + V_j - \epsilon$. When this is true for all j, the

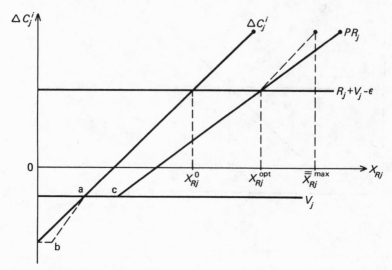

Figure 6-3.

total payment received for units returned $(R_j + V_j)$ will differ because of differences in CFM content and in the reprocessing value V_j, R_j being unaffected by changes in V_j and $\Delta C_j{}^i$. However, when a 100 percent rate is achieved at $R_j < SWTP_j$, optimal R_j as well as optimal refunds per unit of CFM will vary with changes in maximum $\Delta C_j{}^i$ (or ΔC_j) and V_j. The latter variable is assumed to be market-determined and easily observed; thus R_j can be tied to V_j to keep $R_j + V_j$ constant over time until a change in maximum $\Delta C_j{}^i$ (or ΔC_j) requires a change in the sum $R_j + V_j$. Policy cost aspects may, of course, call for less variable refund rates over time and possibly for equalizing R_j over a subgroup of equipment that otherwise would have different optimal refund rates.

Deposit instruments. If the durability of cooling equipment were insignificant, the deposit D_j would simply equal the refund R_j and the return alternative would be open to all discarded units. Since durability in this instance is substantial, two separate issues arise: a deposit–refund system for items sold from now on and the disposal problem for items already in use. Moreover, in dealing with the former issue we have to discuss the deposit rates as something that may deviate from the refund rate owing to the length of time between the two.

Let us assume to begin with that V_j on existing equipment or *SWTP*, or both, during the lifetime of existing equipment are so small that only the future disposal of equipment sold from now on will call for governmental intervention. Thus one possible solution is to calculate an expected optimal R_j at the time of disposal and determine a deposit rate corresponding to this refund rate. With an expected real rate of return on deposits turned over to the government equal to r, the deposit rate would be $D_j = R_j e^{-rt_j}$, where t_j is the expected average lifetime of equipment type j. In this version of the system, the buyer of a piece of cooling equipment would know the real value of the future refund. However, at time t_j the expected R_j at time 0 may not be the appropriate refund rate, given the actual $\Delta C_j{}^i$ and *SWTP* at t_j. If the appropriate refund rate were lower than R_j, R_j would still have to be paid out under a traditional deposit–refund system. But if the appropriate refund rate were higher than R_j, a decision would have to be made on whether to add a (true) subsidy to R_j. With this version of the system, the expected government payments (that is, refunds plus optimal subsidies) will be higher than the value of the deposits at the disposal date in the 100 percent return case.

Another possible solution in the situation now discussed is to separate the actual refund payment completely from the deposit rate actually paid and let the refund be determined as discussed in the preceding section. The refund prospect would then turn from one of a fixed minimum refund rate (adjusted for inflation) to one of a flexible refund rate, that is, one that will bring about an economic stimulus to return instead of dumping cooling equipment at a rate sufficient to meet a given and well-specified policy objective. Thus for any individual year, the refund payments may deviate from the value of the deposits once made for the units involved. But, if we assume that there would be no bias in current estimates of future optimal refund rates, the deposit rate could still be determined as suggested above, and in the long run deposits would tend to cover actual refund payments, even in the 100 percent return case. In this version of the system, however, buyers of cooling equipment would be faced with increased uncertainty about real refund rates.

If this kind of uncertainty were considered a serious burden for buyers, an extreme corrective would be to have the government specify an $R_j + V_j$ in real terms and in advance. Thus buyers of new equipment as well as traders on secondhand markets would know the exact value of this asset. However, because they still would be unaware of the value of $\Delta C_j{}^i$

at the disposal date and because the refund prospect is unlikely to be very high and high enough to cause real concern among buyers, we are not going to pursue this particular alternative further. So, given two alternative versions of a deposit–refund system with the same uniform principle for determining the deposit rate as $D_j = R_j e^{-rt_j}$, we turn to the disposal problem for the existing stock of equipment for which no deposits will have been paid at the purchase date.

Disposal of existing equipment. Given that, in the near future, $SWTP$ and V_j (for existing equipment) are high enough to spur some action concerning disposal problems prior to the disposal of yet unsold equipment, we return to the analysis of optimal refund rates R_j. For R_j to remain a refund rate instead of a pure subsidy rate, owners of existing equipment would have to pay a deposit *ex post,* unconventional as this may seem.

As one extreme alternative, owners of cooling equipment could register their holdings of cooling equipment specified as to age and type at a date when they are already required to report to government, say, in conjunction with income tax returns for households, property tax statements for owners of housing and business property, or registration of automobiles for owners of air-conditioned cars. They would later be billed, and their statements could be checked on a sample basis (with equipment bought after the registration date already carrying a deposit). In contrast to cooling equipment on premises open to the public, refrigerators and freezers in private homes might be technically difficult or legally or morally objectionable to check. Households may therefore be subjected to an assessment on the basis of average holdings; currently, almost all households have a refrigerator and about 50 percent have a freezer.[9] Or as another extreme, the deposit for all equipment could be determined by average holdings, thereby transforming the deposit into an earmarked tax and thus a pure financial instrument.

If an *ex post* deposit solution is not chosen owing to high policy costs or for other reasons, the only way to finance the R_j, at this point a pure subsidy, would be to use other sources of government revenue. Aside from a special one-time tax or the traditional options of raising taxes and reducing other government expenditure, there is the special option of adding a tax for current disposal costs to the deposit D_j collected for new equipment. As we have assumed the deposit rate to be designed, this tax is

---

[9] See Eads and coauthors, *Non-Aerosol Chlorofluorocarbon Emissions,* appendix B.

certain to be socially inefficient. But given that all other financial options open also create inefficiencies (if not, they would already be in use or at least their introduction could not be attributed to the decision to introduce the R_j subsidies), a disposal tax could be an optimal choice given the decision to subsidize proper disposal of cooling equipment.

Finally, the subsidies could be financed by government borrowing, which may have a primary effect of reducing the investment volume in the society. Given that actions taken to reduce CFM emissions in fact are an investment in future environmental quality, borrowing (or, rather, reduction of other investment and hence reduction in future production) is a natural financing alternative. An obvious source of borrowing is the deposit funds accumulating from the sales of new cooling equipment. Thus, instead of being invested in projects giving a real rate of return of r, these funds would partly or wholly be used to finance the R_j subsidies at a capital cost of r. In this way, a part or all of the subsidies and later the refunds R_j would be financed out of current deposits, leaving the final financial decision regarding outstanding refunds, if and when deposits are withdrawn, to future generations.[10]

The special costs of dealing with the disposal problem for existing equipment from introducing *ex post* deposits or financing disposal subsidies by a disposal tax or from other sources, including, for example, borrowing from the deposit funds, will result in a short-term *SWTP* that is systematically below the long-term *SWTP* relevant for returns of new cooling equipment. Thus optimal R_j on existing equipment will tend to be correspondingly lower than discussed earlier or even zero for some or all existing equipment. Furthermore, to avoid an initial overreaction to the return alternative at R_j equal to short-term $SWTP_j$, through an excessive supply from stored-up used equipment, a phasing-in period may be required with gradually rising refund/subsidy rates over time, allowing a steady growth of the reprocessing industry. This possibility as well as the alternative deposit/tax and refund/subsidy paths mentioned above are summed up and illustrated in figure 6-4.

Emissions during use and service of cooling equipment. If emissions from servicing operations have the same impact as emissions from non-return disposal of cooling equipment, the same refund rates could be offered for CFM collected by repairmen. However, in the short-run, when

[10] As we saw in the preceding chapter, the Swedish system for the disposal of hulks has this property.

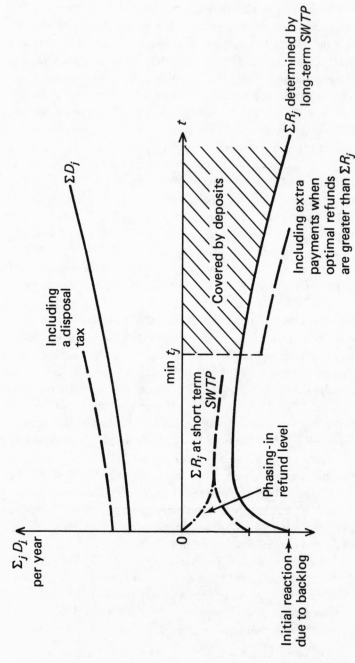

Figure 6-4.

these emissions may be particularly important, a refund rate higher than that for disposal may be called for. This would be true if there were no phasing-in problems for CFM recovered in this pure form. Moreover, it would be true if there were no financial constraints on this kind of refund/subsidy, as would be the case with a deposit (tax) on recharges of CFM. Because the optimal deposit for recharges may be higher than that for initial CFM charges owing to a shorter time to final disposal and because the volume of recharges is certain to exceed the volume of CFM recovered in servicing operations, the total amount of service deposits should be expected to exceed the total amount of service refunds. This might not turn out to be true if other refrigerants with no or smaller expected emission effects and hence smaller deposits could replace CFM with high refund rates. But otherwise, we would expect a surplus to arise that partly or wholly would eliminate the financial problems discussed in the preceding paragraphs.

To sum up, we might expect the deposits and refunds on CFM involved in service operations to be a straightforward application and modification of the rates derived from an analysis of the disposal problem. However, as was indicated earlier, the economic incentive effects may be quite limited in the context of service operations, thus allowing for wide approximations in determining the relevant deposit and refund rates here.

Effects of a Deposit–Refund System

We now turn to look into the main effects of a deposit–refund system along the lines just described. We begin by discussing the effects on disposal behavior—what alternative and when?—as well as the effects on service behavior and on secondhand markets. Then we shift to the market for new equipment, observing the effects on prices, profits, output, and product design. Finally, we try to determine the principal effects on various groups in the economy.

Choice of disposal alternatives. Given the decision to dispose of a piece of cooling equipment and given perfect information on the disposal alternatives (the "return" alternative and the "dumping" alternative), the alternative chosen is simply assumed to be that which minimizes costs, C_d^i or $C_R^i - R - V$ (the subscript for product type j being dropped). For the user, $R + V$ is directly quoted in money, whereas C_R^i and C_d^i may not be. As was indicated earlier, C_R^i is assumed to be the minimum cost of transferring the unit (or the relevant part containing CFM) to the re-processor. In case $C_R{}^i$ is not a transportation cost paid to someone else, it is an imputed cost of the transfer. The cost of the dumping alternative, $C_d{}^i$, is even more likely to be an imputed cost. However, the consumer is not interested in anything more precise than whether the imputed cost difference $C_R{}^i - C_d{}^i$ is larger or smaller than the payment received, $R + V$. Given information from local sellers of new equipment and collectors of used equipment about transportation costs (which may involve a decision on whether to replace the unit with a new one) as well as about the present $R + V$, the consumer simply chooses one of the alternatives, thereby revealing a maximum or minimum imputed cost difference $C_R{}^i - C_d{}^i$. The consumer is assumed to collect this information unless he has reason to believe (say, from the behavior of others) that it does not matter which of the two alternatives he chooses, which we interpret to imply that in fact $C_R{}^i - C_d{}^i \approx R + V$.

Effects on disposal dates. The choice of an optimal disposal date pre-supposes an analysis of what disposal alternative to choose, an analysis which in principle will have to be made continually. The reason is, of course, that the implications of optimal disposal would have to be known before the decision is made on whether to discontinue using (or possibly, servicing) the existing unit. As long as the nonreturn alternative for dis-posal turns out to be optimal, only the effects of higher servicing prices on the choice of disposal date need be considered. But whenever the re-turn alternative is optimal and implies a significant reduction of costs, disposal dates typically will be affected and will be earlier (see the sub-section "The Disposal Decision" in chapter 2). The only general excep-tion is when the unit breaks down and is beyond repair.

To sum up, the introduction of the return alternative may *ceteris paribus* reverse a decision to service the unit—in which case there would have been additional risks of CFM emissions—or reverse a decision to keep the unit in use—in which case there would have been possible net additions to CFM emissions. Thus the fact that the introduction of a return alternative that will be preferred by at least some consumers tends to speed up disposal implies a further reduction in CFM emissions. This is true at least as long as replacements are not sufficiently discouraged by price increases for new equipment due to the deposit.

Effects on servicing behavior. We have just seen that the introduction of a refund on used equipment will tend to reduce demand for servicing.

Now we observe that a deposit introduced on recharges of CFM in used equipment will tend to make service operations more expensive. Although the importance of this effect is in doubt, it will in principle contribute to shifting disposal to an earlier date, regardless of the disposal alternative chosen. Moreover, it will tend to speed up service on equipment suspected to have a CFM leakage. The direction of the short-term effects on the servicing volume is therefore not certain. Nor is it certain to be a positive effect on the recovery behavior by repairmen and the servicing industry. The fact that there is a refund on CFM recovered is in itself a very weak incentive when the refund is to be transferred to the owner.

Effects on secondhand markets. The introduction of a refund will in principle raise the price of secondhand equipment, which now also contains the right to a refund. This effect, however, is likely to be important only for old equipment with a not so distant disposal date, given fairly clear expectations of the size of the future $R + V$ payment. Unless there are structural differences between the supply and the demand side as to the choice of disposal alternative and disposal dates, demand price and supply price will tend to rise to the same extent, leaving the volume traded unchanged.

Not only the refund but also the deposit may have an effect here. Again, both the demand price and the supply price would tend to increase, pushing the equilibrium price up even further.

Effects on the market for new equipment. On the assumption that the product design remains unchanged to begin with, both the refund and the deposit could affect product prices. However, with present durability of cooling equipment, the effect on demand of a refund prospect possibly as late as twenty years from now will be limited. If we took this effect to be zero, it would in fact mean that the refund is discounted much more heavily by the owner than when it is discounted at the government interest rate r, determining the deposit rate. But the depositor's discount rate is likely to exceed r for several reasons. Especially for net borrowers this difference is likely to exist, and it may even be quite large. More important is the possibility that many buyers will simply overlook the fact that there is a refund to be collected some ten or more years from now.

For the type of commodities we are dealing with here, it therefore seems reasonable to assume as an approximation that the refund prospect has no effect on demand but that the deposit has the same effect as an ordinary price increase in the same amount. And with a completely elastic long-term supply, the result will in fact be a price increase equal to the deposit. Given a price elasticity of demand of -0.4 for refrigerators, the effect on output cannot be expected to be very pronounced.

For example, at $r = 0.05$, a \$10 refund (that is, a CFM plus an equipment unit subsidy) in real terms ten to twenty years from now for products now priced at \$200 and up would call for a deposit (equal to the price increase) of \$4 to \$6, or at most 3 percent of the price and hence lead to a long-term reduction in demand for refrigerators by at most 1.2 percent. Moreover, we have to take into account that a large portion of sales are replacements where buyers are simultaneously given a refund on their old equipment. Although this effect on disposable income, in principle, cannot simply be subtracted from the effect on prices, it will at least mitigate the effect on demand from this group. In addition, one possible effect is that refunds and higher servicing costs will speed up replacements (given the price on new equipment) and lead to an increase in demand. The net effect on output and on industry profits is thus likely to be small, in particular with a sufficiently long phasing-in period for the deposit–refund system.

Effects on product design. CFM producers and manufacturers of refrigeration equipment are said to be working constantly on reducing CFM emissions and to have made some progress in this respect.[11] Although the basic reason for this is an effort to improve product performance, it is compatible with the view that current CFM prices have provided some incentive to reduce initial CFM charges and CFM recharges. Deposits on new CFM would add to these incentives, probably to a significant degree. The reason is that refund rates when measured per unit of CFM-containing equipment would have to be relatively high to have any effect at all and hence that refund rates when measured per pound of CFM recovered would be quite substantial. As a possible example, a \$5 refund on automotive air conditioners with an average remaining charge of, say, 2 lb would imply a refund of \$2.50 per pound (recovered CFM here assumed to be uncontaminated and to have $V = 0$). With an average CFM capacity of 4 lb per car, a ten-year average durability, and $r = 0.05$, the deposit would be some \$1.50 per pound or \$6 per unit. This would imply that a deposit would add about 100 percent to the present CFM cost of \$1 to \$2 per pound.[12]

[11] See Du Pont, "Information Requested by EPA," p. III-6.
[12] See Eads and coauthors, *Non-Aerosol Chlorofluorocarbon Emissions,* appendix A.

If the order of magnitude of these figures were realistic, the incentives for design and system changes to reduce CFM emissions would be substantially increased. Eventually, the effects of such a reinforcement of the incentives would be likely to be extensive. Some system changes that now seem to be at an advanced stage of development are as follows: most CFMs could be mixed with leak detectors by which a leakage could be observed by visual inspection, which will facilitate prompt servicing; hermetically sealed automotive air conditioners could replace current non-hermetically-sealed units; on-site repair kits could be used for large refrigeration systems; and F-22 and ammonia could replace F-11 and F-12 in some uses.[13] Furthermore, the durability of products could be changed so that disposal dates and hence remaining emissions at disposal would be delayed or so that non-CFM components would not last as long as they currently do, thereby requiring an early replacement of the unit before leakages appear and possibly making the CFM component re-usable. In addition to changes in product design and servicing procedures, there would be incentives to adjust procedures of manufacturing, storage, and transportation of CFM products as well as intensified R&D of new refrigerants.

Distributional effects. The basis for a *SWTP* > 0 is that there is a non-negligible risk of detrimental repercussions of CFM releases today on the health and environment of future generations. This would mean that there is a nonzero probability that future generations inside as well as outside the policy-active country will benefit from the introduction of an incentive system of the type suggested here.

Focusing on the present generation (at the time of policy implementation) we first of all note that littering of used equipment may be reduced, thus benefiting those who otherwise would have been exposed to the hazards and eyesores of littered units. In addition, we note the effects on different *end users of cooling services:*

1. Those who *discontinue* using a piece of cooling equipment that will not be replaced (including those who sell equipment on the second-hand market and those who have stored or collected discarded equipment) will benefit from the refund option now open to them. This may be true in particular for low-income households with a low $C_R{}^i$, due to low opportunity costs of time.

---

[13] See Du Pont, "Information Requested by EPA."

2. The outcome for those who discard an old piece of equipment to have it *replaced by a new one* may be positive or negative. There is certain to be a price increase on new equipment (given quality), whereas the future benefits of the return alternative are uncertain. Only those who have a $R + V - C_R{}^i + C_d{}^i$ on the now discarded unit that is larger than the deposit on a new unit (assuming the same deposit for all relevant alternatives) are sure to benefit from the system. It should be noted, however, that if optimal real refunds tend to remain fairly constant over time, today's refunds per pound of CFM would tend to be much larger than today's deposits per pound of CFM, given the deposit as a discounted value of the future refund.

3. *First-time buyers* of new equipment would definitely lose by the price increases due to the deposit, assuming (as we have been doing here) that the buyer's discount rate exceeds r in $D = Re^{-rt}$.

4. *Buyers of secondhand equipment* are likely to be confronted with an increase in market prices larger than the present value of the refund prospect, as we have indicated above. Thus this group, which probably contains a large fraction of low-income households, would tend to lose, particularly the first-time buyers among them.

5. Commodities produced by using refrigeration will tend to become more expensive, causing losses to *consumers*. The expansion of industries using refrigeration as an input will be confronted with increased factor prices, and replacements will imply increases in costs. However, the use of refrigeration in manufacturing as well as in the service industry will often involve replacement cycles that are shorter than those for most household uses of refrigeration. Moreover, return disposal, that is, disposal for scrapping and so on, tends to be used more often in this case. Thus refunds will often be a net addition to the income of the firm and appear at an early date, making the present value of the refund nonnegligible. Or these special circumstances for industrial equipment may be such that substantial refunds may not be required, in which case the deposits will be small and have little influence on production costs.

6. To finance refunds (subsidies) on existing equipment, we have discussed solutions in which consumers are taxed. Let us look at the effects on these *taxpayers*. If the tax hits all consumers regardless of holdings of refrigeration equipment, there are certain to be losers, although tax rates will tend to be low. If, at the other extreme, the

tax is levied in relation to such holdings, the gains of those who discontinue holding this kind of equipment will be reduced and perhaps even turn into losses. And it will be less likely now to find net winners among those consumers who have old equipment replaced by new units. In the case in which an excise tax is added to the deposit on new units and the tax is shifted completely on to buyers, the frequency of losers or the size of the losses, or both, will increase among groups (2 through 5). If, however, borrowing (equal to reduced capital formation) is used to finance the refunds on existing equipment, future generations will take the place of present consumers suffering the loss mentioned here.

So far we have discussed effects on consumers. Let us now look at the main effects on producers or *stockholders*. The outcome will to a large extent depend on the phasing-in pattern used. However, part of the negative effects on producers in the field will already have occurred. That is to say, if government is willing to act under present conditions of uncertainty (which the aerosol ban has indicated to be the case), the market should already have registered expected losses from future policy actions and hence some of the costs noted here:

1. The introduction of a deposit–refund system will reduce short-term profits for *CFM producers*. However, the deposit–refund system will lead to an increase in the supply of used CFM, which may benefit this industry to the extent that it is also active in reprocessing. Effects on long-term profits are likely to be negative as well, but the appearance of policy intervention may be considered to have been part of the inevitable long-run uncertainty for the industry, and there is thus a risk of double counting here. Moreover, it should be borne in mind that the industry has the option of reducing negative effects by adopting product changes. *Manufacturers* of cooling equipment will be in a similar position. If policy speeds up replacement of old equipment, however, there will be a demand increase for the products of these manufacturers and possibly for the CFM industry as well.

2. *The repair and servicing industry* may, as we have indicated, be confronted with an uncertain effect on demand for its services. There are factors that tend to favor disposal instead of repair and other factors that increase demand for servicing or shift demand to

an earlier date. The sign of the net effect is therefore difficult to ascertain.

3. We have already touched on the effects on *industries* using refrigeration as an input. (See item 5 in the preceding list.) We have pointed out that short-term cost increases probably would occur because of factor price increases but that in many instances these effects would be small or nonexistent. If not, there would be incentives to make long-run changes in processing techniques and product choice to reduce negative effects on long-run profits.

4. Finally, the *reprocessing industry* dealing with CFM destruction or reclamation will essentially be a new industry, presumably providing benefits for those who engage in it. We have assumed competition to be established here, so long-run profits should tend to zero. To the extent that existing firms are involved in reprocessing and for firms now receiving a larger supply of non-CFM parts of refrigeration equipment, such as scrapping firms, the effect on (short-run) profits would tend to be positive.[14]

Concluding Remarks

We conclude by comparing the deposit–refund system discussed here with the policy of a purely regulatory approach to emission control of refrigerants, an alternative that may look more natural or more attractive to politicians and administrators, at least at first glance. The basic requirement of the regulatory approach is that the producer or seller of a product with potential disposal problems bears responsibility for disposal and takes back the product when the user wants to get rid of it. In a long-

---

[14] As was mentioned earlier, an actual deposit–refund system for cooling equipment in the United States has been outlined elsewhere (see Bohm, "Protecting the Ozone Layer"). There, a refund rate around $2.50 per pound (F-11 and F-12) in 1978 prices was assumed to provide incentives strong enough to put almost all these chemicals appearing in discarded equipment in the hands of a reprocessing industry (for eventual reuse or for other disposal without CFM emissions). Then refunds could be expected to be financed completely by deposits (taxes) on recharges. In fact, total refunds around 1983 would stay on a level below $200 million per year in 1978 prices, whereas total deposits on recharges would be on the order of $300–400 million. Thus neither deposits on new equipment nor extra taxes would be needed to finance the refunds on existing equipment. Instead, the deposits on new equipment could be used in a self-contained system for refunds when this equipment is disposed of in the future.

term market economy perspective, this means that prices will go up and thus that the user will already have paid for the transfer of the liability of legal waste disposal to the producer/seller. Here the rules for proper disposal could be the same as under a deposit–refund system. Thus the producer/seller would either reuse or destroy the returned products himself or send them on to the reprocessing firm that makes the best offer for proper disposal. So the main differences in comparison with the incentive system are (1) that returns have to be made in a specific way, that is, to or via the producer/seller and (2) that no refunds are offered.

Certain problems are connected with this solution, however. First, return costs may be higher owing to the constraints on the form of the transfer of the discarded product. Second, as refunds are ruled out, return rates may be kept at a level that is too low, assuming a significant willingness to make sacrifices for reducing the risks of ozone depletion. This might be true even if the producer/seller were required to pick up the used equipment and this were done in a very smooth way (although incentives for efficient pickup service taken by itself would be lacking) and even if the producer/seller were not allowed to try to sell a new product of his in "exchange" for the old one (although such incentives would definitely exist). Third, and perhaps most important, the product durability of cooling equipment would create problems for this kind of regulatory action. Neither the seller nor the producer may be around when the user eventually wants to dispose of the product, or the user may have moved to a new area, giving rise to prohibitive transportation problems. These two problems would contribute further to low return rates and would probably call for additional measures. Moreover, new producers/sellers will have an advantage over established ones, once the system has been operating for some time. In addition, there will be an incentive to stay in the business for a limited time only (until returns start appearing). Thus there will be detrimental effects on efficiency as well as distributional effects both among sellers/producers and among users.

Some of these problems could be solved by making sellers liable to pick up old units on request regardless of their origin. However, since costs of transportation and handling often would outweigh reuse or resale values, other problems would arise. For example, hidden or overt rebates would be offered on new equipment when there is no "trade-in." This means a return to the original problem, where proper disposal is more costly for the user than improper disposal.

In conclusion, a regulatory return alternative with no economic incentives would limit return rates, possibly to very low levels and possibly much below what a *SWTP* calls for; it will introduce inefficiencies in the markets for new equipment as well as for collecting used equipment; and it would of course have no direct effects on CFM emissions up to the point of disposal. In other words, regulating disposal without the assistance of economic incentives may fail to bring about a satisfactory solution to the emission problems of cooling equipment. In contrast, an economic incentive system of the type discussed here would

- have at least some impact on emissions at all points
- allow return rates to be determined by the revealed social willingness to pay for reductions in the risks of ozone depletion
- not interfere with efficiency in the markets for new equipment or in the collecting and reprocessing markets
- allow costs for refunds/subsidies (in addition to administrative costs) to be covered by deposits/taxes and hence remove the financial problems that might otherwise be used as a rationale for regulation, and
- not seem to have any substantial and politically unattractive distributional effects—especially not against low-income households, for which the payments offered by the return alternative net of the imputed time costs will provide a relatively strong incentive.

This system, which includes a tax (deposit) on CFM used for refrigeration, can be combined with a tax on all CFM uses, if this is (part of) a preferred policy with respect to foam blowing, solvent, and remaining aerosol uses. The tax rate may be the same for all uses—which may require an adjustment of the non-CFM part of the deposit for cooling equipment—or it may differ among uses. The latter approach, though perhaps more cumbersome from an administrative point of view, could be motivated by the fact that different uses have different emission patterns. For example, aerosol use involves a more or less immediate release of all of the CFM contained in the product, whereas refrigerant uses imply a possible CFM release as late as twenty to thirty years after production. Thus it is possible to combine a deposit–refund system for refrigerant uses of CFM with any kind of regulation of such uses as well as with any kind of regulatory or tax scheme for other CFM uses.

AVAILABILITY OF SPARE PARTS: A PROBLEM OF CONSERVATION AND CONSUMER POLICY

A common remark made by critics of the market economy is that model changes and fashion create a waste of resources. Defenders of the market system are quick to point out the advantages of an economy in which innovations are allowed to take place, resulting in model improvements, and consumer interests in fashion are accepted as a real instead of a contrived aspect of consumer welfare. Although net disadvantages to consumers in certain cases are acknowledged, it is argued that these cases are impossible to single out in an objective and effective manner and that overall the free enterprise system produces changes of product design to the benefit of consumers.

If we accept the idea of consumer sovereignty in a market economy and the producer's right to take initiatives in marketing new products as two basic value premises, we might still be interested in investigating ways to avoid cases in which net disadvantages result from model and product changes. In fact, it could be argued that consumers who want to keep their old products in use should be allowed to do so as a part of the consumer sovereignty premise and not be forced to abandon such products because of market failure with respect to repair facilities. From another point of view, there is the merit-want aspect of economic policy, according to which a government may want to reduce raw material or energy "squandering." One or both of these objectives could be implemented partly by a system guaranteeing the availability of spare parts for durable products.

As matters now stand in a market economy, the owner of a durable product of a certain vintage may find that an easily replaceable part cannot be bought. So the product as a whole must be replaced, perhaps by a completely different, and sometimes less preferred, model. Or the existing product can remain in use, but at a low level of effectiveness. Given that the appropriate business calculations have been made, the reason for this situation is that demand for spare parts is too low for them to be marketed at all or made available beyond a certain date, although the product is not yet out of use. The demand could be low because only a few items of the product were ever sold or only a few of them have broken down in a way that would give rise to a demand for spare parts. Although in some cases demand may be sufficiently high for costs to be covered, it may simply be regarded as too "unimportant" for the producer to bother about this market. Or the reason could be linked to consumer information costs, that is, costs for finding out whether the relevant spare parts are available and who is selling them. For older products, these information costs could be substantial and perhaps reflect a situation in which the consumer does not even know where to start looking.

The information cost aspect indicates that an instance of market failure may be involved here. Moreover, it may be one that could be eliminated or reduced by government intervention. Assume, for example, (1) that all producers/importers were required by law to keep spare parts available for a period of time after the product was sold, (2) that this period will be determined by some crude rule taking the "nature of the product" into account, and (3) that the spare parts would have to be delivered within a specified period, or money back. Assume as well some centralized provision of information regarding how and for what price spare parts could be acquired, for example, from catalogs available in post offices. This would create information at least about where to look for statements about available spare parts and about prices of available spare parts. With an arrangement of this kind, taking into account the economies of scale of information activity, markets for spare parts may turn out to be large enough for the required supply of spare parts to be a profitable line of business. If so, we would in fact be dealing with a corrigible market failure.

If government initiatives to organize information as indicated are insufficient for all of the required set of spare parts markets to become profitable, it remains to consider whether the government or the sellers/producers by government decree should subsidize the existence of such markets. This case makes it necessary for us to ask why such an arrangement would at all benefit the economy, that is, its consumers. If consumer demand is not large enough to ensure that the market for spare parts is sustainable without subsidies, we might suspect that it is not in the interest of consumers to sustain these markets. At least, this is the conclusion we would arrive at for a perfect market economy with efficient prices on all markets, no externalities, no economies of scale, and no uncertainty or information gaps concerning either established or new commodities.

However, as we have indicated, we cannot be sure that information regarding the spare parts markets will be perfect in a pure market economy. If some markets for spare parts were self-supporting and others not, the absence of subsidies (in the wide sense implied above) would prevent the latter group of markets from ever appearing. Thus the set of spare parts made available would be incomplete. Consequently, consumers would be uncertain as to whether spare parts were available for a particular model. The smaller the extent of the market for spare parts, the smaller would be the expected return from searching for information about availability or about prices of a particular item, and hence the smaller would be the demand for spare parts. Thus it may be that the only spare parts market able to survive on its own would be a thin one with high information costs.

Thus we have two alternatives: (1) the solution of the pure market economy with relatively few spare parts markets and (2) the solution in which the government by a general or specific decree forces the economy to keep a certain minimum set of such markets and supports the activity in these markets by some information system. In comparing the two alternatives, it may turn out that the consumers' total willingness to pay for spare parts in the latter case can be taken to be so much higher that it would cover all costs for the additional spare parts made available, including those that incur a loss and including the costs of the information system. If so, the second solution would seem to be preferable. (We disregard the possibility that there may be a third—and still better—alternative.)

To sum up the argument so far, we have pointed out that in otherwise perfect market economies the introduction of regulated markets for spare parts could be explained by a market failure in the information system, in the form of economies of scale in information. Aside from this efficiency argument there are the motives of (1) "resource savings" as a merit want and (2) a forced introduction of markets for spare parts as a second-best measure. We know that the latter case may appear in an imperfect market economy with political constraints on pricing, as in, say, systems for reduced energy or raw material consumption as a substitute for higher prices on energy or raw materials. In this particular case, the political constraints may stem from a conviction that low-income households lose by increased prices as compared to alternative measures such as regulation or from a suspicion that plans to raise prices via higher taxes on, say, imported fuels eventually will result in the charging of higher prices by the export cartels to the disadvantage of the importing countries.[15]

[15] In addition, consumer policy objectives may provide a basis for intervention, as it may be considered a basic consumer right to keep expensive products in use to a certain (arbitrary) extent. In particular, the policy makers may have the following two cases in mind: (1) products that otherwise would be taken out of use in

Given these possible reasons for regulation of a minimum set of markets for spare parts, we now turn to an analysis of the consequences of a particular arrangement for establishing such markets. To begin with, we give a set of rules based on the principles of a deposit–refund system for the availability of spare parts. A major reason why a deposit–refund system may be an appropriate instrument for this policy is that in this way it would be possible to maintain—throughout the guarantee period—a situation of *caveat venditor,* that is, an effective future responsibility or liability with the original seller (producer or importer). Without the proper institutions, sellers would be in the position of having the option of leaving the market once the sales of a particular durable product are discontinued, thus avoiding the possibly unprofitable activity of providing the relevant set of spare parts.

A Deposit–Refund System for Availability of Spare Parts

If all durable products were manufactured by big corporations with a long-term commitment to having spare parts available to consumers, as is now the case for major automobile and appliances manufacturers, the need for government intervention would perhaps never arise. In such cases, producers plan to stay in business for a long period of time, and a poor service record today might reduce future demand for the firms' products. Thus the interest of the producer would in these cases coincide with interest of consumers who want to keep old units in use.

All producers of durable products do not show a behavior like that just described. For example, for low-cost durable products—say, appliances, radios, and household utensils priced from $100 down—it is not generally possible now to have broken or worn-out parts replaced by purchases from the producer/seller. Moreover, a requirement for firms to keep spare parts available for some period of time after the durable products were originally sold may well turn out to be an ineffective measure. The result might be a growth of "hit-and-run" producers/sellers who avoid expected net losses of this future service obligation by formal reconstructions so that the liable firms are continuously taken out of business. Thus, in order

---

need of replaceable, inexpensive parts; and (2) products that are liked by or familiar to the consumer and for this reason preferable to new models in spite of the fact that the spare parts required for an extended product life could be made available at high prices only.

to have a workable system, liability would have to be placed more firmly on today's sellers.

One way to achieve a stable system of spare parts availability would be to have the seller put under bond by an amount equal to the value of the commitment required. Before we consider the obviously subtle question of who should require what commitment, it must be pointed out that the bonds could be replaced by bank guarantees or insurance policies, as was suggested earlier (see chapter 4). For major companies with an obvious self-interest in the future availability of spare parts (either because it is a profitable line of business *per se* or because it has important effects on demand for new products), the risk premiums may be quite small, perhaps negligible. But for other sellers, such as small importers from small foreign producers, interest costs or premiums may be substantial. However, proof of a minimum stock of spare parts, including perhaps an option to a subsidiary of the bank or insurance company involved to take over the stock in case of bankruptcy or some similar arrangement, could keep costs down.

Now, who should determine what parts should be available, and for how long and in what amount or percentage of past sales? Taking this question as it is now phrased, we might consider, as one alternative, special courts that would make a detailed specification on the basis of the arguments made by the seller (and his trade association) and a spokesman for a government agency for consumer affairs.[16] The task of these courts would be to make a decision with respect to issues on which the two parties cannot agree. And the decision could be given in the form of a ruling that for a given product sold, n parts (adequately labeled) should be available for at least mail-order delivery during t years or some real compensation should be paid. Some minimum amount of information should be made available, in a standardized form at, say, all post offices.

As an alternative to an *a priori* decision by a court, a statement would be required from an authorized law firm indicating that adequate measures have been taken to protect the consumer interest as given by the law. If and when the adequacy of these measures as well as the corre-

---

[16] The functioning of such courts could resemble that of the special court dealing with cases of deceptive marketing practices and related issues (Marknadsdomstolen) that has operated in Sweden for a decade. For information about this court see, for example, Burton A. Weisbrod, *Public Interest Law—An Economic and Institutional Analysis* (Berkeley, University of California Press, 1978) p. 517.

sponding financial commitment by a bank or insurance company (of the kind represented by Lloyd's in the United Kingdom) later is questioned by consumers, the participation of a government agency and a court will be required, but only then.

To sum up, the law could be so designed that it would force sellers to make a minimum provision of spare parts (or money back), which could imply the buildup of a special stock of parts (to which the firm would have limited access only) but which definitely would involve a financial obligation (for future production of parts or a future compensatory payment). In this way—and with the participation of special courts (or legal experts) and intermediaries such as banks or insurance companies—the deposit–refund system would in general add to the sellers' costs and to consumer prices. If the seller meets his commitments, he will be relieved of his obligations; if not, the firm will lose an amount, for example, a deductible amount to the financial guarantor (the bank or the insurance company), or if the firm is out of business, the whole loss will be made by the guarantor. The system would give buyers an extended ability to have durable products repaired.

The overall benefits of the system now suggested cannot be ascertained unless an attempt has been made to analyze its consequences. The introduction of a law along these lines would give rise to effects on product design, technological change, market structure, and so on. We now turn to a brief outline of what these effects might amount to.

Effects of Spare Part Guarantees

Let us assume at this point that there will be no new goods and no changes of product design for existing goods as a consequence of the introduction of a deposit–refund system for spare parts. Thus, given a set of durable products, we study, first, the effects on the supply of these goods and, second, the effects on the supply of spare parts from the original producer as well as from other sources. In addition, we analyze the effects on the prices of spare parts and of repairs and, finally, the effects on the relevant group of consumers when there is a demand for spare parts but the original seller is out of business. In what follows, we take the seller as identical to the producer of the goods in question.

Supply of individual durable goods. As we have already mentioned, the introduction of the deposit–refund system may in some instances increase expected—fixed as well as variable—costs for the seller of a durable product. This would create a tendency among producers to withdraw certain products from the market. It is possible, however, to imagine the appearance of stimuli working in the opposite direction. The new system would act as a general support of demand for spare parts, which may make certain products profitable to sell owing to a now profitable service/repair/spare part retailing activity. In addition, there may be an increase in demand for products that now will be known to be repairable should they break down. However, these latter effects will probably be small, and thus the net effects will be one of a reduction in the number of durable goods.

Thus even before we discuss the effects on product development (which we may expect to be a reduced set of goods supplied), we should observe a likely trend toward eliminating some of the durable goods that existed initially on account of the cost increases caused by the deposit–refund system. As was indicated earlier, this effect may not be a random one; it may depend on such things as the market structure and product history in different commodity markets. But the general tendency is, as we can see, much like the one we find for many proposals for a more interventionistic consumer policy, that is, higher prices and a smaller set of commodities for consumers to choose from.

Supply of spare parts. Within the initially given set of durable goods, we may expect that the supply of spare parts will increase. To be more specific, we may assume that for a particular model that is still being sold today but was never planned to be sold tomorrow, the producer will now have to make spare parts available tomorrow. This means—in contrast to what we indicated in the preceding paragraph—that there may be an addition to the set of durable products *in use* in the future, that is, products that otherwise would not have been available as secondhand objects or not desired as such. But it also means that there will be a reduction in demand for other models tomorrow, perhaps to the extent that certain models planned for tomorrow will never appear on the market.

The supply of spare parts may come from the original producer (including his original supplier, if the parts were bought from others) or from a special, new producer of spare parts. The original producer is likely to remain as the supplier, especially when the original durable good is still being sold and the parts in question are still being used for new products. When the durable good is withdrawn from the market, the original producer may still be a supplier of the spare parts required by law, either from his own stocks or by a continued production of these parts. If he was the producer of each part as well as the producer of the assembled good, he may continue in this capacity or order quantities from a special producer as demand requires. In other words, it is not necessary that the original producer of a particular part remain the producer of this part.

If the future demand for spare parts could be treated as a deterministic variable, the problem of optimal producer behavior would be relatively simple to resolve. The producer responsible for the supply of spare parts should simply compare increased stocks today with future production from alternative sources as well as with the money-back alternative. Banks and insurance companies would hardly influence producer behavior in the deterministic case. And in a case of uncertain future demand, they would probably not influence the outcome in real terms, if they could be assumed to have access to more or less the same information as the producers. But in the case of uncertain future demand, the optimal behavior for the firm (as well as its creditors) may be to choose a combination of supplies to meet future demand, say, a minimum quantity from stocks and additional quantities to be bought from a special producer.

Depending on the way regulation of spare part supply is designed, there may be effects on the quality of spare parts as well. In principle at least, we could imagine that an obligation to provide spare parts for a particular model might be met by an offer to sell a redesigned, substandard part that involves small costs (and hence small losses, if any) for the seller. To avoid dealing with this contingency here, we assume that the law refers to spare parts of the same quality as provided originally.

Prices of spare parts. As just indicated, we may assume the supply of spare parts to be based on a cost comparison of deliveries from different sources of production. Thus cost efficiency is feasible in this system, at least in principle. However, the seller of the durable product will be put into an unprecedented monopoly position as a seller of spare parts. This means, among other things, that cost efficiency will not be stimulated by competition.[17]

---

[17] Exceptions to this rule could arise, of course, for large spare part markets (compare the market for auto parts). Such markets may, however, exist to a large extent already; thus they may not be relevant to observe in a discussion of spare part markets whose establishment relies on government initiatives.

Another important effect of this monopoly position is of course its effect on price policy. Although the seller may have to accept a competitive price in selling the original durable product, he is free to set his own prices on spare parts. And this situation will probably remain as it is even after an adjustment period. As the experience from the automobile market tells us, there are very few attempts to create competition by standardizing spare parts among different brands or makes (aside from parts like light bulbs and fuses).

Unless the government intervenes in the price formation process as well, consumers will have to accept the monopoly pricing of spare parts. This will of course reduce the consumer benefits of this piece of regulation. In fact, it may conceivably even eliminate the benefits. This is a possible outcome in those cases in which the producer would lose by the introduction of the deposit–refund system, that is, when there would be no future price at which the expected present value of net profits from sales of spare parts would be positive. If so, the seller might try to price the spare parts out of the market, that is, charge prices that would eliminate (practically) all demand for them. This contingency could be avoided, however. One possibility would be to let the seller determine the real price of a part at the time when the original product is being produced and sold, thereby making excessively high prices on spare parts a costly strategy for the seller.

Supply of spare parts in case of seller shutdown. One effect of the deposit–refund system is that a supply of spare parts would appear in product areas where such a supply otherwise would not have existed. Another effect is that the owner of a durable good would be given some protection as to availability of spare parts or compensation for non-availability of spare parts even when the seller has gone bankrupt. The main purpose of introducing a deposit–refund system here is of course to give buyers some protection regardless of whether the seller goes bankrupt or not and to prevent the seller from avoiding his responsibility (as it is defined by law) by going bankrupt as a strategy planned in advance. Still, sellers might withdraw from business and leave some unfulfilled obligations behind.

To deal with the issue of what will happen when the seller leaves his business, let us recall—by reference to figure 6-5—the assumed behavior of a seller remaining in business. For a given period t after production and sales of the original durable good have been discontinued, there may

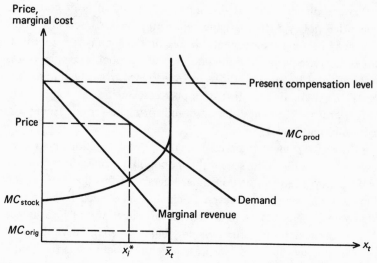

Figure 6-5.

be a given stock $\bar{x}_t$ of a particular spare part. The original marginal cost of production, that is, when the final addition to stocks was made, is indicated by MC_{orig}. The relevant marginal cost of supply from available stocks is given by MC_{stock}, which reflects the expected maximum net value to the seller by keeping one more unit beyond the present period. Depending on the uncertainty of future demand, this net value may increase up to a point determined by expected future demand, expected future production costs for spare parts, and the future compensation level that has been determined. The present compensation level and the present marginal cost of new production (MC_{prod}) are shown in the figure. With a given (expected) demand for period t and an assumed monopoly behavior, sales would amount to x_t^* with new production equal to zero. If stocks had been equal to zero at the beginning of period t or if demand were larger, we would have had some new production (including perhaps a quantity for the purpose of refilling stocks), provided the compensation level were high enough.[18]

Now, what happens when the seller leaves his business in period $t - 1$? It is here that the guarantor—a bank or an insurance company—would enter into the operations on the market for spare parts. Assume

---

[18] Note that the case described here is not necessarily one that is profitable for the seller; the fixed costs of this particular operation may be too high.

first that the seller had a stock of spare parts at the time of the bankruptcy and that the law makes it possible to have these stocks taken over by the guarantor (or a special retail business owned by the guarantor). Let us also assume that new production of spare parts can be bought at a price that is at least as high as MC_{prod} in figure 6-2. This means that in principle the situation would be the same as when the original seller remained in business, with the possible exception of an increase in MC_{prod} (and hence to some extent in MC_{stock}).

Effects on product design. As is the case for all deposit–refund systems, the present one will probably create important incentives for producers to change product design. And as in the other cases we have discussed, it is hard to know specifically what the actual consequences of such incentives will be. Some tendencies toward a slower technical change and longer product durability are expected. Here we try to substantiate these by looking at decisions on whether to release new products already developed as well as at decisions guiding R&D on new products.

Let us look first at how the deposit–refund system for spare part availability will affect firms that are well established in their branch of industry and are in the process of developing or marketing a *new model* of a durable product (such as a household appliance). If the new policy is introduced at a very late stage of this process, there may be no effects at all. But there is likely to be a point in time before which it will be important to consider that the new model will have a more intensive competition than was assumed earlier and, in addition, that this competition will come at least partly from products sold by the same firm. What has happened is of course that the firm has learned that it will have to make spare parts available in the future for the models that it now sells but has planned to have replaced by the new model. Thus, with spare parts being made available to consumers, it can be expected that old models will be kept in use, and demand for the new model will diminish. Other things equal, we may expect that development of some of the new models, somewhere in the process of being designed and marketed, will be stopped or delayed.

Moving on to the case of *new products* that are being developed and marketed when the deposit–refund system makes its future presence known, we note that there may be an effect similar to the one we just discussed. Existing products of the same, or a similar, kind that are sold by other firms will tend to be kept in use for longer periods and hence will increase competition for the new products. If the innovating firm now is selling durable products for which the cross-elasticity of demand with respect to the new product is positive, this tendency will be strengthened. Again, the reason is that competition will arise between the "new" spare parts of the existing products and the new product planned to be sold by the same firm.

So far we have dealt with effects that by themselves increase durability and reduce the rate of product innovation. When we take the indirect effects via R&D activity into account, the picture becomes less clear, however. The producer who is forced to keep spare parts on the market may try to reduce the disadvantages of this system by taking steps aimed at stimulating demand for the spare parts. Or he may try to do exactly the opposite by developing products that are not likely to be repaired.

In order to increase demand for spare parts, the producer may try to develop new models or products that are designed to be more durable on the whole but that rely on the replacement of more expensive (or a greater number of) parts during their "maximal product life." Alternatively, the producer might change product design in order to reduce demand for spare parts in the future. Especially if it is believed that the overall effect of the deposit–refund system would be to impose an unprofitable line of business on the producer, the best remedy might be to eliminate spare parts altogether. This extreme result could be accomplished by eliminating products consisting of replaceable parts. This could be done by making the products all in one piece, for example. Or if the product still is made of parts that in principle are replaceable, the design might aim at making product life end by having the product as a whole fall to pieces (the so-called "one-hoss-shays"). Or the design might aim at having several expensive parts wear out more or less at the same time so that it will never appear worthwhile to have any one part replaced. This kind of evasive behavior could of course jeopardize the assumed net benefits of the policy we have been discussing here. If the risks for such a result were significant, it would be a major argument against this kind of policy.

Summary

A deposit–refund system can be used as an instrument for conservation policy or consumer policy by increasing the availability of spare parts of durable products. From the economist's point of view, it is natural to see the argument for this kind of policy as one of market failure. An essential ingredient in this policy is to ensure the subsistence of such an obligation by producers/sellers through a guarantee bought from banks or insurance companies. A typical agreement between the seller of a product and the guarantor would be for the seller to keep stocks or output capacity for a certain volume of spare parts in addition to paying an insurance fee or interest for protection of consumers in case of seller bankruptcy.

An overall evaluation of this kind of regulation is made complicated by the fact that the composition of products supplied is likely to change, in particular in the long run. Aside from the possible withdrawal of products that existed initially or were planned to be marketed, there will be incentives to adjust product design to stimulate—or deter—future demand for spare parts. If the former tendency dominates, it may be assumed, primarily as a consequence of a reduction of the rate of introduction of new products and new models, that product durability will be longer and the speed of product innovation slower.

For the durable products existing initially and subsequently remaining on the market, the main effect will be a greater availability of spare parts to consumers but at prices reflecting the monopoly position of the producer. The supply of spare parts will, as we have seen, remain the same in principle whether or not the original seller stays in business. That is to say, part of the supply at a given point in time may come from stocks, and part—or the supply as a whole—may come from ongoing production by the original or a new, specialized producer.

INDEX

References to tables are in boldface type

DEPOSIT–REFUND SYSTEMS

Theory and Applications to Environmental, Conservation, and Consumer Policy

"No deposit–No return" may represent efficiency and profits for container manufacturers and supermarkets, but throwaway cans and bottles consume more raw materials than do reusables and they contribute to an obvious litter problem. Hence, the effort in several U.S. states—with Oregon being the pioneer—to pass laws requiring refundable deposits on consumer containers.

Peter Bohm shows that such bottle bills are but one application of deposit–refund systems—economic incentives designed to encourage desirable behavior on the part of business and the public. While primarily theoretical, his book carries the reader from the foundations of deposit–refund systems to some successful examples of their use. Along the way, Bohm shows that such systems can arise naturally in markets as part of